On
Stories
and
Other Essays
on
Literature

BOOKS BY C. S. LEWIS

The Pilgrim's Regress
The Problem of Pain
The Screwtape Letters and Screwtape Proposes a Toast
Broadcast Talks
The Abolition of Man
Christian Behaviour
Beyond Personality
The Great Divorce
George MacDonald: An Anthology
Miracles
Transposition and Other Addresses
Mere Christianity
Surprised by Joy: The Shape of My Early Life
Reflections on the Psalms
The World's Last Night and Other Essays
The Four Loves
Letters to Malcolm: Chiefly on Prayer
Poems
Of Other Worlds: Essays and Stories
Letters of C. S. Lewis
Narrative Poems
A Mind Awake: An Anthology of C. S. Lewis
On Stories: And Other Essays on Literature
Spirits in Bondage: A Cycle of Lyrics
The Business of Heaven: Daily Readings from C. S. Lewis
Present Concerns
All My Road Before Me: The Diary of C. S. Lewis, 1992–1927

For Children

THE CHRONICLES OF NARNIA:
The Lion, the Witch and the Wardrobe
Prince Caspian
The Voyage of the *Dawn Treader*
The Silver Chair
The Horse and His Boy
The Magician's Nephew
The Last Battle

Fiction

Out of the Silent Planet
Perelandra
That Hideous Strength
Till We Have Faces: A Myth Retold
The Dark Tower and Other Stories
Boxen: The Imaginary World of the Young C. S. Lewis

On Stories
and Other Essays
on Literature

C.S. Lewis
Edited by Walter Hooper

A Harvest Book
Harcourt Brace & Company
San Diego   New York   London

Library of Congress Cataloging-in-Publication Data
Lewis, C. S. (Clive Staples), 1898–1963.
On stories, and other essays on literature.
I. Hooper, Walter.   II. Title.
PR6023.E92605   1982   809   81-48014
ISBN 0-15-169964-X   AACR2
ISBN 0-15-668788-7 (Harvest: pbk.)

Printed in the United States of America

First Harvest edition 1982
C D E F G

Contents

Contents

Preface

'You can't get a cup of tea large enough or a book long enough to suit me', said C. S. Lewis; a remark which could almost be used as an epigraph for this short one. He certainly meant what he said, for at that moment I was pouring his tea into a very large Cornish-ware cup and he was reading *Bleak House*.

The theme of the collection is the excellence of Story. And particularly those kinds of story specially dear to Lewis—fairy tales and science fiction. In the essays printed here the author discusses certain literary qualities which he felt critics overlooked, or, the whirligig of fashion being what it is, dismissed too automatically. When most of the pieces were first published in 1966 under the title *Of Other Worlds* (with four stories now reprinted in Lewis's *The Dark Tower and Other Stories*) the most vocal of the literary critics were encouraging readers to find in literature almost everything, life's monotony, social injustice, sympathy with the downtrodden poor, drudgery, cynicism, and distaste: everything except *enjoyment*. Step out of line and you were branded an 'escapist'. It's no wonder that so many people gave up taking their meals in the dining-room and moved into the nether parts of the house—as close as they could get to the kitchen sink.

Lewis heard them, stayed where he was, and proved immune to the whole thing. Hence, the most enduring property of this collection lies with those pieces Lewis wrote about his seven Chronicles of Narnia and his science-fiction trilogy. Still, I have no doubt that our literary gaolers would still have us shackled, in the prison-house of their own making, had not Lewis opened the door, struck off our chains, and led us out. But part of Lewis's effectiveness as liberator lay in the fact that he was familiar with the interior of the gaol-house from his own earlier imprisonment. Let's consider what put him there and how he escaped.

C. S. Lewis can't have been more than five or six years old when he wrote, in a notebook he much later passed on to me, a story called 'To Mars and Back' and another little romance about chivalrous mice and rabbits riding out in full armour to kill cats. While his interest in romance, particularly of the fantastic and 'other worldly' kinds, remained with him all his life, it is perhaps more than coincidence that when his mother died in 1908, though he was only nine years old, his compositions began to reflect more and more the interests and 'grown-up' talk of his father, who was a police court solicitor in Belfast.

Lewis was later to say in his autobiography, *Surprised by Joy*, that what drove him to write was an extreme manual clumsiness owing to the inherited deformity of having only one joint in the thumb. That is one thing. But the evidence of the sheer pleasure he found in writing suggests that this proclivity would have been about as difficult to stifle as it would be to reverse the rotation of the earth.

Most of the as yet unpublished stories Lewis began when he was about six and continued till he was about fifteen were, at first, about his imaginary world of Animal-Land and the an-thropomorphic beasts which inhabit it. In time his elder brother, Warren, selected India as 'his' country. Then, in order that it might be a shared world, India was lifted out of its place in the real world and set alongside Animal-Land—the two thus becom-ing, in time, the single state of Boxen. Soon the maps of Boxen included the principal train and steamship routes—one of War-ren's contributions. The capital city of Murray even had its own newspaper. And so, out of an attic full of commonplace children's toys and ink pots, there emerged a world almost as consistent and self-sufficient as one finds in Trollope's Barsetshire novels.

As early legends of King Arthur and his Court grew to include romances of individual knights of the Round Table, so a systematic reading of the Boxen stories—profusely illustrated by Lewis's pen and covering over seven hundred years—reveals a similar kind of growth. The young lad's interest was, at first, that of a historian of Boxen: as time went on he turned to writing novels and biographies in which the principal characters spring into prominence. Lewis's masterpiece is Lord John Big. This noble frog is already the Little-Master, *i.e.*, the Prime Minister, when we meet him in 'Boxen: Or Scenes from Boxonian City Life' (written in 1912). Later he has his own biography: 'The Life of Lord John Big of Bigham' in three 'volumes' or exercise books, composed in 1913.

There is much to admire about Boxen. Lord Big is a frog of immense personality, and I find him almost as unforgettable as Reepicheep the Mouse and Puddleglum the Marsh-wiggle of the Narnian stories (who were, as Lewis told me, his favourites). There is nothing to suggest that the author had to labour to find 'filling' for his carefully constructed plots. And the humour, though more constrained than that we find in the works he wrote years later, is unmistakably of the Lewis kind. He had been training himself, without knowing it, to be a novelist.

But, as Lewis himself admitted in *Surprised by Joy*, Boxen is empty of poetry and romance. I think it might astonish the reader of the Narnian books to know just how prosaic it is. In fairness, it ought to be pointed out that this was partly intentional, for as Lewis was later to say: 'When I began writing stories in exercise books I tried to put off all the things I really wanted to write about till at least the second page—I thought it wouldn't be like a grown-up book if it became interesting at once.'* Most of all, the Boxen stories are blighted by, of all things, politics— something which Lewis came to detest in later life. It did, after all, hold him so long in bondage. The characters in 'Scenes from Boxonian City Life' all relish a place in the 'Clique', though none of them—and certainly not the author—appears to have any clear idea what a clique is. This is not surprising, for as Lewis wanted his characters to be 'grown up', he naturally interested them in

---

* 'Christianity and Culture,' *Christian Reflections*, ed. Walter Hooper (1967).

what he knew to be 'grown-up' affairs. And politics, as both Lewis and his brother told me, was a topic they heard a great deal of from their father and his contemporaries.

As Boxen came to an end, there began what Lewis was to look back upon as the happiest period of his life. It started in the autumn of 1914 when he was sent to Little Bookham in Surrey to be 'crammed' for Oxford by an old family friend, W. T. Kirkpatrick. A rationalist, Kirkpatrick, almost certainly without any intention of doing so, strengthened the atheistic beliefs Lewis already held. Coincidental with his going to Little Bookham, Lewis met a Belfast neighbour, Arthur Greeves, who was to become his life-long friend and, after Warren, his closest confidant—the perfect sharer of his taste in literature. One has only to glance through Lewis's weekly exchange of letters with Arthur* to see the growth of his imagination as it revels in the vigour of legend in Malory's *Morte d'Arthur*, William Morris's *The Well at the World's End*, and George MacDonald's *Phantastes*, which work was to become for Lewis almost the ideal of what a romance should be and one which he claimed 'baptised' his imagination. This 'baptism' was not seen to be such at the time, and the 'holiness' he found in *Phantastes* and other works of MacDonald took some years to find its way through Lewis's truculent resistance to Christianity. What Lewis was passionately interested in sharing with Arthur was the kind of stories which were weird, fantastic, beautiful, expressions of great 'myths'—and most decidedly *not* those concerned with 'everlasting problems'—by which he meant all that goes under the undeserved name of 'realism'.

Lewis's first term in Oxford, his brief friendship with a fellow member of the Officers' Training Corps, Paddy Moore, which led to his promise to look after Paddy's mother should he survive the trenches of France during World War I, his return to Oxford after the war (in which Paddy was killed), and his 'adoption' of Mrs. Moore—all are sufficiently dealt with in *They*

---

*They Stand Together: The Letters of C. S. Lewis to Arthur Greeves (1914–1963), ed. Walter Hooper (1979).

Stand Together and *C. S. Lewis: A Biography*.* What concerns us here are the events which caused Lewis to shift this way and that until he emerged as the author of the kind of stories he liked so much, but which he eventually had to write himself.

As far back as 1912, when he lost his belief in Christianity, Lewis became subject to an occasional attraction to and repulsion from the occult. During his undergraduate years at Oxford; while sharing accommodations with his adopted mother Mrs. Moore, he met two people who caused him to recoil. One of them was an 'old, dirty, gabbling, tragic Irish parson' in whom a 'ravenous desire for personal immortality co-existed . . . with (apparently) a total indifference to all that could, on a sane view, make immortality desirable'.† The other, once a practising psycho-analyst, was a close connection whom Lewis spent weeks nursing, and who had been driven mad from 'flirting with Theosophy, Yoga, Spiritualism, Psychoanalysis, what not?'‡ Lewis liked both men. However, the corrupting influence of Spiritualism on them, the 'New Psychology' which was causing many people to become foolishly and cheaply introspective—all this decided Lewis against anything that wavered towards the occult. His repulsion is evident in his diary. Looking for something to steady his mind, he recorded on the 19th January 1927 the reassurance he found in turning back to the poetry of Wordsworth: 'That's the real imagination, no bogies, no Karmas, no gurus, no damned psychism there. I have been astray among second rate ideas too long.' Thereafter Lewis shunned all thoughts about immortality and even all that sort of romanticism which had once been one of the chief pleasures and concerns of his life.

Until, that is, he came under the altogether benign influence of a fellow don at Oxford, Professor J. R. R. Tolkien. Not only was Tolkien a Christian, but, as Lewis explained in a letter to Greeves, one of the human carriers of the Faith to him. The actual event took place on the evening of the 19th September 1931,

---

*By Roger Lancelyn Green and Walter Hooper.
†*Surprised by Joy: The Shape of My Early Life* (1955), ch. XIII.
‡*Ibid*.

when Lewis, Tolkien, and another friend, Hugo Dyson, were up all night discussing 'myth' and its relation to the revelation of God in Christ. Tolkien, like Lewis, had long feasted on ancient myths, particularly those of Norse origin. The difference between them was that while Lewis defined myths as 'lies breathed through silver', Tolkien—already at work on his vast invented world of Middle Earth—believed in the inherent *truth* of mythology. 'Just as speech is invention about objects and ideas', he said to Lewis that same evening, 'so myth is invention about truth. We have come from God, and inevitably the myths woven by us, though they contain error, will also reflect a splintered fragment of the true light, the eternal truth that is with God. Indeed only by myth-making, only by becoming a "sub-creator" and inventing stories, can Man ascribe to the state of perfection that he knew before the Fall.'*

This was to be one of the biggest shakings up Lewis had ever known, and thereafter as much a part of his philosophy and theology as it was of Tolkien's. Indeed, so immediate was the impression, that Lewis in his account of it to Greeves on the 18th October 1931 was able to admit that the 'story of Christ is simply a true myth: a myth working on us in the same way as the others, but with this tremendous difference that *it really happened*.'

Whether the reader of Lewis's books is or is not a Christian, it ought to be said here that Lewis's conversion just *was* the chief watershed in his life. There was no nook or cranny of his being that it did not eventually reach and transform. Without it I am confident that he would never have become the good and great man he was. That he would have been a writer of some note was already evident: but without the conversion his one-time rampant ambition would not have been enough. I do not know about others. But for Lewis and *his* ambition, it was very like a man living with a beast with only enough food for one. And the beast wants it all. As it turned out, First Things found their proper place and secondary things remained where they should.

And where, in literature, should First Things be put? As expected, Lewis placed his reliance on imaginary worlds. A long-

---

*Humphrey Carpenter, *J. R. R. Tolkien: A Biography* (1977), ch. IV.

time admirer of what used to be called 'scientifiction', he felt it a serious defect that most stories of 'other worlds' should be used as vehicles for exalting some of man's most selfish tendencies. It was to be some time before he created anything like a 'mythology' of his own, but we have it on his own authority that his interplanetary romances and his Narnian stories all began with 'seeing pictures' in his mind. Never, he claims, did he *begin* with a 'message' or a 'moral', but that these things pushed their own way in during the process of writing.

Lewis was at the time of that momentous conversation with Tolkien at work on *The Allegory of Love: A Study in Medieval Tradition*. My guess is that some of the mental 'pictures' which were later to lead him to write a story set on Mars—*Out of the Silent Planet*—may have resulted from his study of Bernardus Silvestris's rare twelfth-century account of creation, *De Mundi Universitate*.* I see from his carefully annotated copy, now in my possession, that he finished reading it on the 4th August 1930. That he was impressed by Bernardus's mention of the 'Oyarses'— the ruling essence or tutelary Spirit of a planet—is evident from his extensive marginalia. In any case, wishing to know more about the 'Oyéresu' (Lewis's name for more than one Oyarses) and their relation to allegory as it was to be defined in *The Allegory of Love*, he wrote—probably shortly after the talk with Tolkien—to C. C. J. Webb, a former professor of the philosophy of the Christian religion. Professor Webb was fascinated by medieval problems and in his reply of the 31st October 1931 (still in Lewis's copy of the book) he pointed out that 'Oyarses' was a corruption of *Ousiarches*, as found in Pseudo-Apuleius's *Asclepius* (xix). Those who have read *The Allegory of Love* will find a mention of the author's debt to Webb in the appendix on 'Genius and Genius'. And those who have not will presumably have met Lewis's beautifully imagined planetary Intelligences or Archangels in his *Out of the Silent Planet*, indeed, in chapter XXII,

---

*Edited by C. S. Barach and J. Wrobel, it was published in Innsbruck in 1876. After 102 years there has (finally) appeared a new edition of this same work, entitled *Cosmographia*, edited by Peter Dronke. It has been translated into English by Winthrop Wetherbee as *The 'Cosmographia' of Bernardus Silvestris* (1973).

under the guise of fiction, there are specific references to the Oyarses of Bernardus, as well as one 'C. J.', who is of course C. C. J. Webb.

Lewis's completion of *The Allegory of Love* in 1935 coincided almost exactly with his discovery of David Lindsay's *Voyage to Arcturus* (1920). Most people are put off by Lindsay's ghastly and unhallowed story. Lewis himself thought that it was on the borderline of the diabolical, but he was immensely grateful for what he learned from it. Writing to Ruth Pitter, the poet, on the 4th January 1947, he said: 'From Lyndsay I first learned what other planets in fiction are really good for; for *spiritual* adventures. Only they can satisfy the craving which sends our imaginations off the earth. Or putting it another way, in him I first saw the terrific results produced by the union of the kinds of fiction hitherto kept apart: the Novalis, G. Macdonald, James Stephens sort and the H. G. Wells, Jules Vernes sort. My debt to him is very great.'

I can hear the shrill voices of some for whom Lewis has become a 'subject' rather than a superb story-teller reminding me that he paid other tributes to Lindsay's book and that he cited *other* reasons for writing the first of his interplanetary novels. Well, so he did. But to my mind this only confirms what he wrote in 'It All Began with a Picture ... ' about the inspiration behind some of his fiction. 'I don't believe', he said, 'anyone knows exactly how he "makes things up". Making up is a very mysterious thing. When you "have an idea" could you tell anyone exactly *how* you thought of it?'

The mistake is to suppose that Lewis was under the most compelling oath to tell 'exactly how it happened', after he has already confessed that he cannot speak with such exactness. It is clear that when he did try to account for the different impulses which went into his story-writing one factor seemed specially vivid at one time, another specially vivid at some other—that *all* throw light on this mysterious process of 'inspiration'. It is better to see them as parts of a whole rather than contradictions of one another.

For instance, in replying to Roger Lancelyn Green's inquiry about the impetus behind *Out of the Silent Planet*, Lewis said in a letter of the 28th December 1938: 'What immediately spurred me to write was Olaf Stapledon's *Last and First Men* and an essay ['The Last Judgment'] in J. B. S. Haldane's *Possible Worlds*, both of which seems to take the idea of such travel seriously and to have the desperately immoral outlook which I try to pillory in Weston. I like the whole planetary idea as a *mythology* and simply wished to conquer for my own (Christian) point of view what has always been used by the opposite side.'

Further light is shed by his answer to Sister Penelope of the 9th August 1939 in which he wrote: 'What set me about writing the book was the discovery that a pupil of mine took all that dream of interplanetary colonisation quite seriously, and the realisation that thousands of people in one form or another depend on some hope of perpetuating and improving the human species for the whole meaning of the universe—that a "scientific" hope of defeating death is a real rival to Christianity. ... I believe this great ignorance might be a help to the evangelisation of England: any amount of theology can be smuggled into people's minds under cover of romance without their knowing it.'

Except for his academic works, Lewis never wrote more than a single draft of his novels, which indeed suggests that the stories were worked out in his head before he put pen to paper. And it seems in this case that the final impetus which produced his first words on the page was a kind of bargain or wager he made with Tolkien early in 1937. Writing about it some years later, Tolkien recalled: 'Lewis said to me one day: "Tollers, there is too little of what we really like in stories. I am afraid we shall have to write some ourselves."'* Tolkien did not in fact complete the story he began, but Lewis kept his part of the bargain and sometime between the spring and autumn of 1937 he wrote *Out of the Silent Planet*. Lewis told me that he did not at this time foresee his other science-fiction novels. It wasn't long, however, before other 'pictures' began forming in his mind, resulting in *Perelandra* (1943) and *That Hideous Strength* (1945), which make up his interplanetary trilogy. The one-time heady attraction exercised upon him by 'other worlds' had been resolved. And of this he was

---

*Humphrey Carpenter, *The Inklings* (1978), ch IV.

later to write, 'My own planetary romances have been not so much the gratification of that fierce curiosity as its exorcism.'

And so it was that Lewis strode out of the prison of 'realism'. Not by any self-conscious 'daring' or attempted 'originality', but by writing what it had been given him to say. There was at the time the expected flutter about a distinguished medievalist prostituting his talents and great learning on the highly suspect field of science fiction. But this significant contribution to the new mythology carried an inner weight which none of the so-called realists even dared to approach. And, really, at the bottom of all this, lay a little lad's desire to play in an imaginary world of Boxen. For again, from back over the years, it was as if Boxen was returning to him. Certainly the desire to construct these 'other worlds' had seized him now as never before, and came, perforce, trailing glory.

The way was now open for Narnia—that beloved outpouring of everlasting charity. Typical of Lewis, the 'childishness' of these books was presented with anything but apologies. In the fourth essay in this book, written in 1952, Lewis said, 'When I was ten, I read fairy tales in secret and would have been ashamed if I had been found doing so. Now that I am fifty I read them openly. When I became a man I put away childish things, including the fear of childishness and the desire to be very grown up.' The essays which follow are surely evidence for this.

It is a pleasure to record my gratitude to Mr. Owen Barfield and Dr. Barbara Reynolds for much valuable advice on the editing of this book. I should point out that, except for the first, fourth, fifth, sixth, seventh, eighth, ninth, nineteenth, and twentieth pieces, which appeared in *Of Other Worlds*, all the others are here published in book form for the first time.

'On Stories' was first published in *Essays Presented to Charles Williams* in 1947. It was originally read, in a slightly fuller form, to a Merton College undergraduate literary society on the 14th November 1940 as 'The Kappa Element in Romance'. 'Kappa' is taken from κρυπτόν and means the 'hidden element'.

'The Novels of Charles Williams' was written at the request of the British Broadcasting Corporation, and Lewis read it over the Third Programme of the BBC on the 11th February 1949. It has never been published before and, indeed, had lain undetected in the BBC Written Archives until I came across it quite by accident in 1980. I am indebted to the British Broadcasting Corporation for permission to publish it here.

The novels of E. R. Eddison—*The Worm Ouroboros* (1922), *Styrbion the Strong* (1926), *Mistress of Mistresses* (1935), *A Fish Dinner in Memison* (1941), and the posthumous *Mezentian Gate* (1958)—were to become an indispensable part of Lewis's library after his discovery of *The Worm Ouroboros* in 1942. This led to a friendship between the two men, and it may have been Lewis's rapturous enthusiasm for Eddison's romances which led to their publication in paperback in New York in 1968. While we could wish it much longer, this 'Tribute to E. R. Eddison' (written some years before it was printed on the dust jacket of *The Mezentian Gate*) is too good to ignore and for that reason is reproduced here.

'On Three Ways of Writing for Children' was read to the Library Association and published in their *Proceedings, Papers and Summaries of Discussions at the Bournemouth Conference 29th April to 2nd May 1952*.

'Sometimes Fairy Stories May Say Best What's to Be Said' first appeared in *The New York Times Book Review* of 18 November 1956.

'On Juvenile Tastes' is reprinted from the *Church Times, Children's Book Supplement*, 28 November 1958.

'It all Began with a Picture...' is reprinted here from the *Radio Times,* 15 July 1960.

'On Science Fiction', a talk given to the Cambridge University English Club on the 24th November 1955, appeared first in *Of Other Worlds*, as did 'A Reply to Professor Haldane', which is a rejoinder to Professor J. B. S. Haldane's article 'Auld Hornie, F. R. S.', in the *Modern Quarterly* of Autumn 1946, in which essay he criticises Lewis's science-fiction trilogy. Professor Haldane, a theoretical biologist, was at once a disillusioned Marxist and violently anti-Christian. I have not thought it necessary to reprint Haldane's article, for Lewis makes the argument quite clear. Besides, the chief value of Lewis's reply is not in its polemical nature, but in the valuable light he throws on his own books.

'The Hobbit' is Lewis's review of his friend Tolkien's book of the same title, and the review is taken from *The Times Literary Supplement* of 2 October 1937.

'Tolkien's *Lord of the Rings*' is a combination of two reviews about Tolkien's great trilogy. The first portion of this piece appeared as 'The Gods Return to Earth' in *Time and Tide*, 14 August 1954, and the second was published as 'The Dethronement of Power', also in *Time and Tide*, 22 October 1955. Professor Tolkien told me that he had been reading various genealogies and appendices to Lewis long before there was any written story. His interests, he told me, were primarily in those aspects of 'Middle Earth' and that it was his friend C. S., or 'Jack', Lewis who encouraged him to write a story to go with them. 'You know Jack', he said to me. 'He had to have a *story*! And that story—*The Lord of the Rings*—was written to keep him quiet!' It is, as it was meant to be, a generous and telling tribute.

When his friend Dorothy L. Sayers died in December 1957, Lewis was asked to write a panegyric for the memorial service to be held for her at St. Margaret's Church, London, on the 15th January 1958. Lewis was unable to attend the service, and his composition was read by the Lord Bishop of Chichester (George Bell). Following Lewis's death, I was one of those who began searching for the unpublished panegyric—a piece of writing which seemed determined to elude discovery. Indeed, it was not until this book was about to go to the printers that Miss Sayers's son, Anthony Fleming, came to my rescue with the rather messy typescript which had been made for the Bishop to read from. Then, glory of glories, a further search uncovered the 'real thing'. Finally, best of all was the day when Mr. Fleming and I sat in the drawing room of the Athenaeum Club in London, reading the original manuscript—which Lewis had given him after the memorial service. I am most deeply grateful to Mr. Fleming for solving what his talented mother might have called 'The Case of the Missing Panegyric'—and I hope it will prove as enjoyable *found* as it was desired when lost.

'The Mythopoeic Gift of Rider Haggard' is my title for Lewis's review of Morton Cohen's biography of Haggard. It appeared under the title 'Haggard Rides Again' in *Time and Tide*, 3 September 1960.

'George Orwell' is taken from *Time and Tide* of 8 January 1955.

'The Death of Words' was originally published in *The Spectator*, 22 September 1944.

'The Parthenon and the Optative' was Lewis's title for the essay which appeared without one in the section 'Notes on the Way', of *Time and Tide*, 11 March 1944.

'Period Criticism' was Lewis's own title for the essay in 'Notes on the Way', *Time and Tide*, 9 November 1946.

'Different Tastes in Literature' is the title I have given Lewis's 'Notes on the Way' as it appeared in two parts in *Time and Tide* of 25 May 1946 and 1 June 1946.

'On Criticism', written fairly late in the author's life, appeared first in *Of Other Worlds*. 'Unreal Estates' is an informal conversation about science fiction between Lewis, Kingsley Amis and Brian Aldiss. It was recorded on tape by Brian Aldiss in Lewis's rooms in Magdalene College, Cambridge, on the 4th December 1962. It was first published as 'The Establishment must die and rot...' in *SF Horizons*, Spring 1964 and later as 'Unreal Estates' in *Encounter*, March 1965.

Readers should know that the person to whom this book is dedicated is Lady Collins of Collins Publishers, London. The idea of making the collection was hers, and when the Trustees of the Lewis Estate learned of her plans to retire in October 1981 it seemed right that it should be offered to her. Lady Collins has for many years been in charge of Collins's Religious Books, and it is primarily through the Fontana Series that she has introduced C. S. Lewis to most of those who now read him. In my long friendship with Lady Collins I have found so much to admire that every effort to praise her falls short of what is adequate. The author of the Proverbs expressed it much better in saying 'Let her own works praise her'.

Oxford   WALTER HOOPER

On
Stories
and
Other Essays
on
Literature

On
Stories

It is astonishing how little attention critics have paid to Story considered in itself. Granted the story, the style in which it should be told, the order in which it should be disposed and (above all) the delineation of the characters, have been abundantly discussed. But the Story itself, the series of imagined events, is nearly always passed over in silence, or else treated exclusively as affording opportunities for the delineation of character. There are indeed three notable exceptions. Aristotle in the *Poetics* constructed a theory of Greek tragedy which puts Story in the centre and relegates character to a strictly subordinate place. In the Middle Ages and the early Renaissance, Boccaccio and others developed an allegorical theory of Story to explain the ancient myths. And in our own time Jung and his followers have produced their doctrine of Archetypes. Apart from these three attempts the subject has been left almost untouched, and this has had a curious result. Those forms of literature in which Story exists merely as a means to something else—for example, the novel of manners where the story is there for the sake of the characters, or the criticism of social conditions—have had full justice done to them; but those forms in which everything else is there for the sake of the story have been given little serious attention. Not only have they been despised, as if they were fit only for children, but even the kind of pleasure they give has, in my opinion, been misunderstood. It is the second injustice which

3

I am most anxious to remedy. Perhaps the pleasure of Story comes as low in the scale as modern criticism puts it. I do not think so myself, but on that point we may agree to differ. Let us, however, try to see clearly what kind of pleasure it is: or, rather, what different kinds of pleasure it may be. For I suspect that a very hasty assumption has been made on this subject. I think that books which are read merely 'for the story' may be enjoyed in two very different ways. It is partly a division of books (some stories can be read only in the one spirit and some only in the other) and partly a division of readers (the same story can be read in different ways).

What finally convinced me of this distinction was a conversation which I had a few years ago with an intelligent American pupil. We were talking about the books which had delighted our boyhood. His favourite had been Fenimore Cooper whom (as it happens) I have never read. My friend described one particular scene in which the hero was half-sleeping by his bivouac fire in the woods while a Redskin with a tomahawk was silently creeping on him from behind. He remembered the breathless excitement with which he had read the passage, the agonised suspense with which he wondered whether the hero would wake up in time or not. But I, remembering the great moments in my own early reading, felt quite sure that my friend was misrepresenting his experience, and indeed leaving out the real point. Surely, surely, I thought, the sheer excitement, the suspense, was not what had kept him going back and back to Fenimore Cooper. If that were what he wanted any other 'boy's blood' would have done as well. I tried to put my thought into words. I asked him whether he were sure that he was not over-emphasising and falsely isolating the importance of the danger simply as danger. For though I had never read Fenimore Cooper I had enjoyed other books about 'Red Indians'. And I knew that what I wanted from them was not simply 'excitement'. Dangers, of course, there must be: how else can you keep a story going? But they must (in the mood which led one to such a book) be Redskin dangers. The 'Redskinnery' was what really mattered. In such a scene as my friend had described, take away the feathers, the high cheek-bones, the whiskered trousers, substitute a pistol for a

4

tomahawk, and what would be left? For I wanted not the momentary suspense but that whole world to which it belonged—the snow and the snow-shoes, beavers and canoes, warpaths and wigwams, and Hiawatha names. Thus I; and then came the shock. My pupil is a very clear-headed man and he saw at once what I meant and also saw how totally his imaginative life as a boy had differed from mine. He replied that he was perfectly certain that 'all that' had made no part of his pleasure. He had never cared one brass farthing for it. Indeed—and this really made me feel as if I were talking to a visitor from another planet—in so far as he had been dimly aware of 'all that', he had resented it as a distraction from the main issue. He would, if anything, have preferred to the Redskin some more ordinary danger such as a crook with a revolver.

To those whose literary experiences are at all like my own the distinction which I am trying to make between two kinds of pleasure will probably be clear enough from this one example. But to make it doubly clear I will add another. I was once taken to see a film version of *King Solomon's Mines*. Of its many sins—not least the introduction of a totally irrelevant young woman in shorts who accompanied the three adventurers wherever they went—only one here concerns us. At the end of Haggard's book, as everyone remembers, the heroes are awaiting death entombed in a rock chamber and surrounded by the mummified kings of that land. The maker of the film version, however, apparently thought this tame. He substituted a subterranean volcanic eruption, and then went one better by adding an earthquake. Perhaps we should not blame him. Perhaps the scene in the original was not 'cinematic' and the man was right, by the canons of his own art, in altering it. But it would have been better not to have chosen in the first place a story which could be adapted to the screen only by being ruined. Ruined, at least, for me. No doubt if sheer excitement is all you want from a story, and if increase of dangers increases excitement, then a rapidly changing series of two risks (that of being burned alive and that of being crushed to bits) would be better than the single prolonged danger of starving to death in a cave. But that is just the point. There must be a pleasure in such stories distinct from mere excitement or I should not feel that I had been cheated in being given the earthquake instead of Haggard's actual scene. What I lose is the whole sense of the deathly (quite a different thing from simple danger of death)—the cold, the silence, and the surrounding faces of the ancient, the crowned and sceptred, dead. You may, if you please, say that Rider Haggard's effect is quite as 'crude' or 'vulgar' or 'sensational' as that which the film substituted for it. I am not at present discussing that. The point is that it is extremely different. The one lays a hushing spell on the imagination; the other excites a rapid flutter of the nerves. In reading that chapter of the book curiosity or suspense about the escape of the heroes from their death-trap makes a very minor part of one's experience. The trap I remember for ever: how they got out I have long since forgotten.

It seems to me that in talking of books which are 'mere stories'—books, that is, which concern themselves principally with the imagined event and not with character or society— nearly everyone makes the assumption that 'excitement' is the only pleasure they ever give or are intended to give. *Excitement*, in this sense, may be defined as the alternate tension and appeasement of imagined anxiety. This is what I think untrue. In some such books, and for some readers, another factor comes in.

To put it at the very lowest, I know that something else comes in for at least one reader—myself. I must here be autobiographical for the sake of being evidential. Here is a man who has spent more hours than he cares to remember in reading romances, and received from them more pleasure perhaps than he should. I know the geography of Tormance better than that of Tellus. I have been more curious about travels from Uplands to Utterbol and from Morna Moruna to Koshtra Belorn than about those recorded in Hakluyt. Though I saw the trenches before Arras I could not now lecture on them so tactically as on the Greek wall, and Scamander and the Scaean Gate. As a social historian I am sounder on Toad Hall and the Wild Wood or the cave-dwelling Selenites or Hrothgar's court or Vortigern's than on London, Oxford, and Belfast. If to love Story is to love excitement then I ought to be the greatest lover of excitement alive. But the fact is that what is said to be the most 'exciting' novel in the world, *The Three Musketeers*, makes no appeal to me at all. The total lack of atmosphere repels me. There is no country in the book—save as a storehouse of inns and ambushes. There is no weather. When they cross to London there is no feeling that London differs from Paris. There is not a moment's rest from the 'adventures': one's nose is kept ruthlessly to the grindstone. It all means nothing to me. If that is what is meant by Romance, then Romance is my aversion and I greatly prefer George Eliot or Trollope. In saying this I am not attempting to criticise *The Three Musketeers*. I believe on the testimony of others that it is a capital story. I am sure that my own inability to like it is in me a defect and a misfortune. But that misfortune is evidence. If a man sensitive and perhaps over-sensitive to Romance likes least that Romance which is, by common consent, the most 'exciting' of all, then it follows that 'excitement' is not the only kind of pleasure to be got out of Romance. If a man loves wine and yet hates one of the strongest wines, then surely the sole source of pleasure in wine cannot be the alcohol?

If I am alone in this experience then, to be sure, the present essay is of merely autobiographical interest. But I am pretty sure that I am not absolutely alone. I write on the chance that some others may feel the same and in the hope that I may help them to clarify their own sensations.

In the example of *King Solomon's Mines* the producer of the film substituted at the climax one kind of danger for another and thereby, for me, ruined the story. But where excitement is the only thing that matters kinds of danger must be irrelevant. Only degrees of danger will matter. The greater the danger and the narrower the hero's escape from it, the more exciting the story will be. But when we are concerned with the 'something else' this is not so. Different kinds of danger strike different chords from the imagination. Even in real life different kinds of danger produce different kinds of fear. There may come a point at which fear is so great that such distinctions vanish, but that is another matter. There is a fear which is twin sister to awe, such as a man in war-time feels when he first comes within sound of the guns; there is a fear which is twin sister to disgust, such as a man feels on finding a snake or scorpion in his bed-room. There are taut, quivering

7

fears (for one split second hardly distinguishable from a kind of pleasurable thrill) that a man may feel on a dangerous horse or a dangerous sea; and again, dead, squashed, flattened, numbing fears, as when we think we have cancer or cholera. There are also fears which are not of *danger* at all: like the fear of some large and hideous, though innocuous, insect or the fear of a ghost. All this, even in real life. But in imagination, where the fear does not rise to abject terror and is not discharged in action, the qualitative difference is much stronger.

I can never remember a time when it was not, however vaguely, present to my consciousness. *Jack the Giant-Killer* is not, in essence, simply the story of a clever hero surmounting danger. It is in essence the story of such a hero surmounting *danger from giants*. It is quite easy to contrive a story in which, though the enemies are of normal size, the odds against Jack are equally great. But it will be quite a different story. The whole quality of the imaginative response is determined by the fact that the enemies are giants. That heaviness, that monstrosity, that un-couthness, hangs over the whole thing. Turn it into music and you will feel the difference at once. If your villain is a giant your orchestra will proclaim his entrance in one way: if he is any other kind of villain, in another. I have seen landscapes (notably in the Mourne Mountains) which, under a particular light, made me feel that at any moment a giant might raise his head over the next ridge. Nature has that in her which compels us to invent giants: and only giants will do. (Notice that Gawain was in the north-west corner of England when 'etins aneleden him', giants came *blowing* after him on the high fells. Can it it be an accident that Wordsworth was in the same places when he heard 'low breathings coming after him'?) The dangerousness of the giants is, though important, secondary. In some folk-tales we meet giants who are not dangerous. But they still affect us in much the same way. A *good* giant is legitimate: but he would be twenty tons of living, earth-shaking oxymoron. The intolerable pressure, the sense of something older, wilder, and more earthy than humanity, would still cleave to him.

But let us descend to a lower instance. Are pirates, any more than giants, merely for threatening the hero? That sail which is rapidly overhauling us may be an ordinary enemy: a Don or a Frenchman. The ordinary enemy may easily be made just as lethal as the pirate. At the moment when she runs up the Jolly Roger, what exactly does this do to the imagination? It means, I grant you, that if we are beaten there will be no quarter. But that could be contrived without piracy. It is not the mere increase of danger that does the trick. It is the whole image of the utterly lawless enemy, the men who have cut adrift from all human society and become, as it were, a species of their own—men strangely clad, dark men with earrings, men with a history which they know and we don't, lords of unspecified treasure in undiscovered islands. They are, in fact, to the young reader almost as mythological as the giants. It does not cross his mind that a man—a mere man like the rest of us—might be a pirate at one time of his life and not at another, or that there is any smudgy frontier between piracy and privateering. A pirate is a pirate, just as a giant is a giant.

Consider, again, the enormous difference between being shut out and being shut in: if you like, between agoraphobia and claustrophobia. In *King Solomon's Mines* the heroes were shut in: so, more terribly, the narrator imagined himself to be in Poe's *Premature Burial*. Your breath shortens while you read it. Now remember the chapter called 'Mr Bedford Alone' in H. G. Wells's *First Men in the Moon*. There Bedford finds himself shut out on the surface of the Moon just as the long lunar day is drawing to its close—and with the day go the air and all heat. Read it from the terrible moment when the first tiny snowflake startles him into a realisation of his position down to the point at which he reaches the 'sphere' and is saved. Then ask yourself whether what you have been feeling is simply suspense. 'Over me, around me, closing in on me, embracing me ever nearer was the Eternal . . . the infinite and final Night of space.' That is the idea which has kept you enthralled. But if we were concerned only with the question whether Mr Bedford will live or freeze, that idea is quite beside the purpose. You can die of cold between Russian Poland and new Poland, just as well as by going to the Moon, and the pain will be equal. For the purpose of killing Mr Bedford 'the infinite and final Night of space' is almost entirely otiose: what is by cosmic standards an infinitesimal change of temperature is sufficient to kill a man and absolute zero can do no more. That airless outer darkness is important not for what it can do to Bedford but for what it does to us: to trouble us with Pascal's old fear of those eternal silences which have gnawed at so much religious faith and shattered so many humanistic hopes: to evoke with them and through them all our racial and childish memories of exclusion and desolation: to present, in fact, as an intuition one permanent aspect of human experience.

And here, I expect, we come to one of the differences between life and art. A man really in Bedford's position would probably not feel very acutely that sidereal loneliness. The immediate issue of death would drive the contemplative object out of his mind: he would have no interest in the many degrees of increasing cold lower than the one which made his survival impossible. That is one of the functions of art: to present what the narrow and desperately practical perspectives of real life exclude.

I have sometimes wondered whether the 'excitement' may not be an element actually hostile to the deeper imagination. In inferior romances, such as the American magazines of 'scientific-tion' supply, we often come across a really suggestive idea. But the author has no expedient for keeping the story on the move except that of putting his hero into violent danger. In the hurry and scurry of his escapes the poetry of the basic idea is lost. In a much milder degree I think this has happened to Wells himself in the *War of the Worlds*. What really matters in this story is the idea of being attacked by something utterly 'outside'. As in *Piers Plowman* destruction has come upon us 'from the planets'. If the Martian invaders are merely dangerous—if we once become mainly concerned with the fact that they can *kill* us—why, then, a burglar or a bacillus can do as much. The real nerve of the romance is laid bare when the hero first goes to look at the newly fallen projectile on Horsell Common. 'The yellowish-white metal that gleamed in the crack between the lid and the cylinder had an unfamiliar hue. *Extra-terrestrial* had no meaning for most of the onlookers.' But *extra-terrestrial* is the key word of the whole story. And in the later horrors, excellently as they are done, we lose the feeling of it. Similarly in the Poet Laureate's *Sard Harker* it is the journey across the Sierras that really matters. That the man who has heard that noise in the cañon—'He could not think what it was. It was not sorrowful nor joyful nor terrible. It was great and strange. It was like the rock speaking'—that this man should be later in danger of mere murder is almost an impertinence.

It is here that Homer shows his supreme excellence. The landing on Circe's island, the sight of the smoke going up from amidst those unexplored woods, the god meeting us ('the messenger, the slayer of Argus')—what an anti-climax if all these had been the prelude only to some ordinary risk of life and limb! But the peril that lurks here, the silent, painless, unendurable change into brutality, is worthy of the setting. Mr de la Mare too has surmounted the difficulty. The threat launched in the opening paragraphs of his best stories is seldom fulfilled in any identifiable event: still less is it dissipated. Our fears are never, in one sense, realised: yet we lay down the story feeling that they, and far more, were justified. But perhaps the most remarkable achievement in this kind is that of Mr David Lindsay's *Voyage to Arcturus*. The experienced reader, noting the threats and promises of the opening chapter, even while he gratefully enjoys them, feels sure that they cannot be carried out. He reflects that in stories of this kind the first chapter is nearly always the best and reconciles himself to disappointment; Tormance, when we reach it, he forbodes, will be less interesting than Tormance seen from the Earth. But never will he have been more mistaken. Unaided by any special skill or even any sound taste in language, the author leads us up a stair of unpredictables. In each chapter we think we have found his final position; each time we are utterly mistaken. He builds whole worlds of imagery and passion, any one of which would have served another writer for a whole book, only to pull each of them to pieces and pour scorn on it. The physical dangers, which are plentiful, here count for nothing: it is we ourselves and the author who walk through a world of spiritual dangers which makes them seem trivial. There is no recipe for writing of this kind. But part of the secret is that the author (like Kafka) is recording a lived dialectic. His Tormance is a region of the spirit.

He is the first writer to discover what 'other planets' are really good for in fiction. No merely physical strangeness or merely spatial distance will realise that idea of otherness which is what we are always trying to grasp in a story about voyaging through space: you must go into another dimension. To construct plausible and moving 'other worlds' you must draw on the only real 'other world' we know, that of the spirit.

Notice here the corollary. If some fatal progress of applied science ever enables us in fact to reach the Moon, that real journey will not at all satisfy the impulse which we now seek to gratify by writing such stories. The real Moon, if you could reach it and survive, would in a deep and deadly sense be just like anywhere else. You would find cold, hunger, hardship, and danger; and after the first few hours they would be *simply* cold, hunger, hardship, and danger as you might have met them on Earth. And death would be simply death among those bleached craters as it is simply death in a nursing home at Sheffield. No man would find an abiding strangeness on the Moon unless he were the sort of man who could find it in his own back garden. 'He who would bring home the wealth of the Indies must carry the wealth of the Indies with him.'

Good stories often introduce the marvellous or supernatural, and nothing about Story has been so often misunderstood as this. Thus, for example, Dr Johnson, if I remember rightly, thought that children liked stories of the marvellous because they were too ignorant to know that they were impossible. But children do not always like them, nor are those who like them always children; and to enjoy reading about fairies—much more about giants and dragons—it is not necessary to believe in them. Belief is at best irrelevant; it may be a positive disadvantage. Nor are the marvels in good Story ever mere arbitrary fictions stuck on to make the narrative more sensational. I happened to remark to a man who was sitting beside me at dinner the other night that I was reading Grimm in German of an evening but never bothered to look up a word I didn't know, 'so that it is often great fun' (I added) 'guessing what it was that the old woman gave to the prince which he afterwards lost in the wood'. 'And specially difficult in a fairy tale,' said he, 'where everything is arbitrary and therefore the object might be anything at all.' His error was profound. The logic of a fairy tale is as strict as that of a realistic novel, though different.

Does anyone believe that Kenneth Grahame made an arbitrary choice when he gave his principal character the form of a toad, or that a stag, a pigeon, a lion, would have done as well? The choice is based on the fact that the real toad's face has a grotesque resemblance to a certain kind of human face—a rather apoplectic face with a fatuous grin on it. This is, no doubt, an accident in the sense that all the lines which suggest the resemblance are really there for quite different biological reasons. The ludicrous quasi-human expression is therefore changeless: the toad cannot stop grinning because its 'grin' is not really a grin at all. Looking at the creature we thus see, isolated and fixed, an aspect of human vanity in its funniest and most pardonable form; following that hint Grahame creates Mr Toad—an ultra-Johnsonian 'humour'. And we bring back the wealth of the Indies; we have henceforward more amusement in, and kindness towards, a certain kind of vanity in real life.

But why should the characters be disguised as animals at all? The disguise is very thin, so thin that Grahame makes Mr Toad on one occasion 'comb the dry leaves out of his *hair*'. Yet it is quite indispensable. If you try to rewrite the book with all the characters humanised you are faced at the outset with a dilemma. Are they to be adults or children? You will find that they can be neither. They are like children in so far as they have no responsibilities, no struggle for existence, no domestic cares. Meals turn up; one does not even ask who cooked them. In Mr Badger's kitchen 'plates on the dresser grinned at pots on the shelf'. Who kept them clean? Where were they bought? How were they delivered in the Wild Wood? Mole is very snug in his subterranean home, but what was he living *on*? If he is a *rentier* where is the bank, what are his investments? The tables in his forecourt were 'marked with rings that hinted at beer mugs'. But where did he get the beer? In that way the life of all the characters is that of children for whom everything is provided and who take everything for granted. But in other ways it is the life of adults. They go where they like and do what they please, they arrange their own lives.

To that extent the book is a specimen of the most scandalous escapism: it paints a happiness under incompatible conditions— the sort of freedom we can have only in childhood and the sort we can have only in maturity—and conceals the contradiction by the further pretence that the characters are not human beings at all. The one absurdity helps to hide the other. It might be expected that such a book would unfit us for the harshness of reality and send us back to our daily lives unsettled and discontented. I do not find that it does so. The happiness which it presents to us is in fact full of the simplest and most attainable things—food, sleep, exercise, friendship, the face of nature, even (in a sense) religion. That 'simple but sustaining meal' of 'bacon and broad beans and a macaroni pudding' which Rat gave to his friends has, I doubt not, helped down many a real nursery dinner. And in the same way the whole story, paradoxically enough, strengthens our relish for real life. This excursion into the preposterous sends us back with renewed pleasure to the actual.

It is usual to speak in a playfully apologetic tone about one's adult enjoyment of what are called 'children's books'. I think the convention a silly one. No book is really worth reading at the age of ten which is not equally (and often far more) worth reading at the age of fifty—except, of course, books of information. The only imaginative works we ought to grow out of are those which it would have been better not to have read at all. A mature palate will probably not much care for *crème de menthe*: but it ought still to enjoy bread and butter and honey.

Another very large class of stories turns on fulfilled prophecies—the story of Oedipus, or *The Man Who Would Be King*, or *The Hobbit*. In most of them the very steps taken to prevent the fulfilment of the prophecy actually bring it about. It is foretold that Oedipus will kill his father and marry his mother. In order to prevent this from happening he is exposed on the mountain: and that exposure, by leading to his rescue and thus to his life among strangers in ignorance of his real parentage, renders possible both the disasters. Such stories produce (at least in me) a feeling of

awe, coupled with a certain sort of bewilderment such as one
often feels in looking at a complex pattern of lines that pass over
and under one another. One sees, yet does not quite see, the
regularity. And is there not good occasion both for awe and
bewilderment? We have just had set before our imagination
something that has always baffled the intellect: we have *seen* how
destiny and free will can be combined, even how free will is the
modus operandi of destiny. The story does what no theorem can
quite do. It may not be 'like real life' in the superficial sense: but
it sets before us an image of what reality may well be like at some
more central region.

It will be seen that throughout this essay I have taken my
examples indiscriminately from books which critics would (quite
rightly) place in very different categories—from American 'scientifiction' and Homer, from Sophocles and *Märchen*, from children's stories and the intensely sophisticated art of Mr de la Mare.
This does not mean that I think them of equal literary merit. But
if I am right in thinking that there is another enjoyment in Story
besides the excitement, then popular romance even on the lowest
level becomes rather more important than we had supposed.
When you see an immature or uneducated person devouring what
seem to you merely sensational stories, can you be sure what kind
of pleasure he is enjoying? It is, of course, no good asking *him*. If
he were capable of analysing his own experience as the question
requires him to do, he would be neither uneducated nor
immature. But because he is inarticulate we must not give
judgement against him. He may be seeking only the recurring
tension of imagined anxiety. But he may also, I believe, be
receiving certain profound experiences which are, for him, not
acceptable in any other form.

Mr Roger Lancelyn Green, writing in *English* not long ago,
remarked that the reading of Rider Haggard had been to many a
sort of religious experience. To some people this will have seemed
simply grotesque. I myself would strongly disagree with it if
'religious' is taken to mean 'Christian'. And even if we take it in a
sub-Christian sense, it would have been safer to say that such
people had first met in Haggard's romances elements which they
would meet again in religious experience if they ever came to have

any. But I think Mr Green is very much nearer the mark than those who assume that no one has ever read the romances except in order to be thrilled by hair-breadth escapes. If he had said simply that something which the educated receive from poetry can reach the masses through stories of adventure, and almost in no other way, then I think he would have been right. If so, nothing can be more disastrous than the view that the cinema can and should replace popular written fiction. The elements which it excludes are precisely those which give the untrained mind its only access to the imaginative world. There is death in the camera.

As I have admitted, it is very difficult to tell in any given case whether a story is piercing to the unliterary reader's deeper imagination or only exciting his emotions. You cannot tell even by reading the story for yourself. Its badness proves very little. The more imagination the reader has, being an untrained reader, the more he will do for himself. He will, at a mere hint from the author, flood wretched material with suggestion and never guess that he is himself chiefly making what he enjoys. The nearest we can come to a test is by asking whether he often *re-reads* the same story.

It is, of course, a good test for every reader of every kind of book. An unliterary man may be defined as one who reads books once only. There is hope for a man who has never read Malory or Boswell or *Tristram Shandy* or Shakespeare's *Sonnets*: but what can you do with a man who says he 'has read' them, meaning he has read them once, and thinks that this settles the matter? Yet I think the test has a special application to the matter in hand. For excitement, in the sense defined above, is just what must disappear from a second reading. You cannot, except at the first reading, be really curious about what happened. If you find that the reader of popular romance—however uneducated a reader, however bad the romances—goes back to his old favourites again and again, then you have pretty good evidence that they are to him a sort of poetry.

The re-reader is looking not for actual surprises (which can come only once) but for a certain surprisingness. The point has often been misunderstood. The man in Peacock thought that he had disposed of 'surprise' as an element in landscape gardening when he asked what happened if you walked through the garden for the second time. Wiseacre! In the only sense that matters the surprise works as well the twentieth time as the first. It is the *quality* of unexpectedness, not the *fact* that delights us. It is even better the second time. Knowing that the 'surprise' is coming we can now fully relish the fact that this path through the shrubbery doesn't *look* as if it were suddenly going to bring us out on the edge of the cliff. So in literature. We do not enjoy a story fully at the first reading. Not till the curiosity, the sheer narrative lust, has been given its sop and laid asleep, are we at lesiure to savour the real beauties. Till then, it is like wasting great wine on a ravenous natural thirst which merely wants cold wetness. The children understand this well when they ask for the same story over and over again, and in the same words. They want to have again the 'surprise' of discovering that what seemed Little Red Riding Hood's grandmother is really the wolf. It is better when you know it is coming: free from the shock of actual surprise you can attend better to the intrinsic surprisingness of the *peripeteia*.

I should like to be able to believe that I am here in a very small way contributing (for criticism does not always come later than practise) to the encouragement of a better school of prose story in England: of story that can mediate imaginative life to the masses while not being contemptible to the few. But perhaps this is not very likely. It must be admitted that the art of Story as I see it is a very difficult one. What its central difficulty is I have already hinted when I complained that in the *War of the Worlds* the idea that really matters becomes lost or blunted as the story gets under way. I must now add that there is a perpetual danger of this happening in all stories. To be stories at all they must be series of events: but it must be understood that this series—the *plot*, as we call it—is only really a net whereby to catch something else. The real theme may be, and perhaps usually is, something that has no sequence in it, something other than a process and much more like a state or quality. Giantship, otherness, the desolation of space, are examples that have crossed our path. The titles of some stories illustrate the point very well. *The Well at the World's End*— can a man write a story to that title? Can he find a series of events following one another in time which will really catch and fix and bring home to us all that we grasp at on merely hearing the six words? Can a man write a story on Atlantis—or is it better to leave the word to work on its own? And I must confess that the net very seldom does succeed in catching the bird. Morris in *The Well at the World's End* came near to success—quite near enough to make the book worth many readings. Yet, after all, the best moments of it come in the first half.

But it does sometimes succeed. In the works of the late E. R. Eddison it succeeds completely. You may like or dislike his invented worlds (I myself like that of *The Worm Ouroboros* and strongly dislike that of *Mistress of Mistresses*) but there is here no quarrel between the theme and the articulation of the story. Every episode, every speech, helps to incarnate what the author is imagining. You could spare none of them. It takes the whole story to build up that strange blend of renaissance luxury and northern hardness. The secret here is largely the style, and especially the style of the dialogue. These proud, reckless, amorous people create themselves and the whole atmosphere of their world chiefly by talking. Mr de la Mare also succeeds, partly by style and partly by never laying the cards on the table. Mr David Lindsay, however, succeeds while writing a style which is at times (to be frank) abominable. He succeeds because his real theme is, like the plot, sequential, a thing in time, or quasi-time: a passionate spiritual journey. Charles Williams had the same advantage, but I do not mention his stories much here because they are hardly pure story in the sense we are now considering. They are, despite their free use of the supernatural, much closer to the novel; a believed religion, detailed character drawing, and even social satire all come in. *The Hobbit* escapes the danger of degenerating into mere plot and excitement by a very curious shift of tone. As the humour and homeliness of the early chapters, the sheer 'Hobbitry', dies away we pass insensibly into the world of epic. It is as if the battle of Toad Hall had become a serious *heimsökn* and Badger had begun to talk like Njal. Thus we lose one theme but find another. We kill—but not the same fox.

It may be asked why anyone should be encouraged to write a form in which the means are apparently so often at war with the end. But I am hardly suggesting that anyone who can write great poetry should write stories instead. I am rather suggesting what those whose work will in any case be a romance should aim at. And I do not think it unimportant that good work in this kind, even work less than perfectly good, can come where poetry will never come.

Shall I be thought whimsical if, in conclusion, I suggest that this internal tension in the heart of every story between the theme and the plot constitutes, after all, its chief resemblance to life? If Story fails in that way does not life commit the same blunder? In real life, as in a story, something must happen. This is just the trouble. We grasp at a state and find only a succession of events in which the state is never quite embodied. The grand idea of finding Atlantis which stirs us in the first chapter of the adventure story is apt to be frittered away in mere excitement when the journey has once been begun. But so, in real life, the idea of adventure fades when the day-to-day details begin to happen. Nor is this merely because actual hardship and danger shoulder it aside. Other grand ideas—home-coming, reunion with a beloved—similarly elude our grasp. Suppose there is no disappointment; even so—well, you are here. But now, something must happen, and after that something else. All that happens may be delightful: but can any such series quite embody the sheer state of being which was what we wanted? If the author's plot is only a net, and usually an imperfect one, a net of time and event for catching what is not really a process at all, is life much more? I am not sure, on second thoughts, that the slow fading of the magic in *The Well at the World's End* is, after all, a blemish. It is an image of the truth. Art, indeed, may be expected to do what life cannot do: but so it has done. The bird has escaped us. But it was at least entangled in the net for several chapters. We saw it close and enjoyed the plumage. How many 'real lives' have nets that can do as much?

In life and art both, as it seems to me, we are always trying to catch in our net of successive moments something that is not successive. Whether in real life there is any doctor who can teach us how to do it, so that at last either the meshes will become fine enough to hold the bird, or we be so changed that we can throw our nets away and follow the bird to its own country, is not a question for this essay. But I think it is sometimes done—or very, very nearly done—in stories. I believe the effort to be well worth making.

The Novels of Charles Williams

One of the silliest critical remarks on record was made by Leigh Hunt when he complained that the *Lays of Ancient Rome* lacked the true poetical aroma of the *Faerie Queene*. There is this to be said for him, that he made it not only in a letter, but in a begging letter, to Macaulay himself; and, as Macaulay acknowledged to Napier, that was a manly act.* But as criticism it is deplorable. I have sometimes wondered whether certain criticisms on the stories of Charles Williams are not equally wide of the mark.

The complaint often made against them is that they mix what some people call the realistic and the fantastic. I would rather fall back on an older critical terminology and say that they mix the Probable and the Marvellous. We meet in them, on the one hand, very ordinary modern people who talk the slang of our own day, and live in the suburbs: on the other hand, we also meet the supernatural—ghosts, magicians, and archetypal beasts. The first thing to grasp is that this is not a mixture of two literary kinds. That is what some readers suspect and resent. They acknowledge, on the one hand, 'straight' fiction, the classical novel as we know it from Fielding to Galsworthy. They acknowledge, on the other, the pure fantasy which creates a world of its own, cut off in a kind of ring fence, from reality; books like *The*

*Letter to Macvey Napier of 16 November 1842 in *The Letters of Thomas Babington Macaulay*, ed. Thomas Pinney (1977).

Wind in the Willows or *Vathek* or *The Princess of Babylon*, and they complain that Williams is asking them to skip to and fro from the one to the other in the same work. But Williams is really writing a third kind of book which belongs to neither class and has a different value from either. He is writing that sort of book in which we begin by saying 'Let us suppose that this everyday world were, at some one point, invaded by the marvellous. Let us, in fact, suppose a violation of frontier.'

The formula is of course no novelty. Even in childhood most of us who are now fifty had learned very clearly the difference in kind between a fairy tale by Grimm and a fairy tale by E. Nesbit. The one transported you to a new world with its own laws and its own characteristic inhabitants. But the whole point of the other was that it supposed Tottenham Court Road or a dingy lodging house to be suddenly invaded by a phoenix or an amulet. The ordinary and, in that sense, classical ghost story does the same thing; the realistic and mundane character of the scene and persons is an essential part of the effect. So, in a far subtler way, Mr de la Mare pours his bottomless misgivings over the very world we all know. *Dr Jekyll and Mr Hyde* intrudes its strange horror upon surroundings studiously prosaic. F. Anstey for his comic marvels builds realistic nests. Even the *Alice* books and the *Gulliver* books owe much to the matter-of-fact and resolutely unimaginative nature of their principal characters. If Alice were a princess, if Gulliver were a romantic voyager or even a philosopher, the effect would be destroyed. Now if this literary kind is permissible at all, it is surely idle to complain that it mixes two literary levels, the realistic and the fantastic. On the contrary, it keeps its own level throughout: that level on which we suppose that a violation of frontier has occurred in the actual world.

Now some people doubt whether the kind is permissible. Of what value, it may be asked, are such supposals? And one answer to that question I myself would rule out at once. They are not allegories. I hasten to add that it is almost impossible to make a story of this kind, or of any kind, which the reader cannot turn into an allegory if he chooses. Everything in art and most things in Nature can be allegorised if you are determined to do it: as the history of medieval thought shows. But I do not think that is how such stories were written nor how they ought to be read. The starting point is a supposal. 'Suppose I found a country inhabited by dwarfs. Suppose two men could exchange bodies.' Nothing less, but equally nothing more, is demanded. And now, what is the point of it?

For some of us, of course, the question hardly arises. Such supposing appears to us the inalienable right and inveterate habit of the human mind. We do it all day long: and therefore do not see why we should not do it, at times, more energetically and consistently, in a story. But for those others who feel that it needs justification, I think a justification can be found.

Every supposal is an ideal experiment: an experiment done with ideas because you can't do it any other way. And the function of an experiment is to teach us more about the things we experiment on. When we suppose the world of daily life to be invaded by something other, we are subjecting either our conception of daily life or our conception of that other, or both, to a new test. We put them together to see how they will react. If it succeeds, we shall come to think, and feel, and imagine more accurately, more richly, more attentively, either about the world which is invaded or about that which invades it, or about both. And here, of course, we come to the great division between writers of this kind.

Some are experimenting solely on the world of daily life: others are experimenting on the invader as well. It depends partly on their literary choice, but partly on their philosophy. Some people, of course, do not believe that there is a potential invader. For them the sole purpose of supposing an invasion must be to throw light on our daily and normal experience. Others, who believe that there is a possible invader, can (though it is not necessary that they always should) expect light on it also to flow from the supposal. Hence we get two kinds of invasion story. *Vice Versa* is a perfect example of the first. The only function of the Garuda Stone is to put Mr Bultitude and Dr Grimstone and the rest in an otherwise impossible relation in order that we may watch their reactions. So in *Dr Jekyll and Mr Hyde*. The machinery whereby the two selves are separated is some trumpery about draughts and powders in which Stevenson hardly invites our interest: what matters is the result. Comic, or strongly ethical, authors usually adopt this method. Mr de la Mare is at the other extreme. His achievement is to awake 'thoughts beyond the reaches of our souls', to bring home to us the precariousness of our common-sense world, and to share with us his own disquieting consciousness of that which, on his view, it conceals. 'Supposing', he says, 'this concealment, never very efficient, broke down completely for a few hours.'

Now Williams is at the same end of the scale as Mr de la Mare. I do not mean that they are in any other respect alike. In the quality of their imagination they are as different as possible: Mr de la Mare's world is one of half-lights and silence and distances, a dusk 'washed with silver', whereas Williams's is one of blazing colours, hard outlines, and bell-like resonance. You would look in vain in Williams for the delicacy, the immense importance of what is not said, which delights us in Mr de la Mare: you would be equally disappointed if you searched Mr de la Mare for the aquiline energy, the pomp, the gaiety, the orgiastic quality, of Williams. But in this one respect they are alike; each, having supposed a violation of frontier, is interested in both sides of the frontier.

No doubt, the first and simplest approach to Williams's stories is to note and enjoy the lights which they cast on this side of the frontier, on our normal experience. His story *The Place of the Lion** seems to me to throw a light which I dare not neglect on the world that I myself chiefly inhabit, the academic world. The heroine, Damaris Tighe, is an extreme example of the complacent researcher. She is studying medieval philosophy and it has never once occurred to her that the objects of medieval thought might have any reality. As Williams tells us, she regarded Abelard and St Bernard as the top form in a school of which she was not so much the headmistress as the inspector. Then comes the supposal. How if those objects were, after all, real? How if they began to manifest themselves? How if this research-beetle had to experience what it so glibly catalogued? Even those who do not feel at

---

**The Place of the Lion* (1931), *All Hallows' Eve* (1945), *Descent into Hell* (1937).

the end of the book that we know any more about the Platonic Forms may well feel that we know more about ourselves as researchers—have seen, as if from outside, the fatuous assumption of superiority which will certainly dominate all our thinking about the past if we take no measures to correct it.

So again in *All Hallows' Eve* the strange sufferings to which Betty is subjected disengage for us her quite possible, yet now seldom imagined, character of wholly undefended and incorruptible innocence. To put it in another way, I find that when I read her history the word *victim*, after so many years of commonplace usage, is restored in my mind to its ancient, sacred and sacrificial dignity, and my vision of the everyday world proportionately sharpened.

That, indeed, is only one instance of a curious effect which Williams's supposals often have. They render possible the creation of good characters. Good characters in fiction are the very devil. Not only because most authors have too little material to make them of, but because we as readers have a strong subconscious wish to find them incredible. Notice how cleverly Scott gets under our guard by making Jeanie Deans inferior to us in everything except her virtues. That gives us our sop: we are taken off our guard. In Williams we are similarly off our guard. We see his good people in strange circumstances and do not think much of calling them good. Only on later reflection do we discover what we have been surprised into accepting.

I will go back to that point in a moment. Meantime I must repeat the claim or the confession (whichever you call it) that this illumination of the ordinary world is only one half of a Williams story. The other half is what he tells us about a different world. To the strict Materialist who believes unshakeably that there is no such thing, I suppose this cannot be more than a curiosity or material for psychoanalysis. Frankly, Williams is not addressing such readers. But, of course, neither is he addressing only his coreligionists. Indeed, explicitly or exclusively Christian conceptions are not often put before us. What have we then? At the lowest, one man's guess about unknowable things. But all who do not from the outset rule out the very possibility of those things will perhaps admit that one man may guess better than another.

And if we think a man is guessing very well indeed we begin to doubt whether 'guessing' is the right word.

I would hesitate to claim that Williams was a mystic. If a mystic means one who follows the negative way by rejecting images, then he was, consciously and deliberately, the very reverse. The choice between the two ways, the legitimacy, the dignity, and the danger, of both, is one of his favourite themes. But I am convinced that both the content and the quality of his experience differed from mine and differed in ways which oblige me to say that he saw further, that he knew what I do not know. His writing, so to speak, brings me where I have never gone on my own sail or steam; and yet that strange place is so attached to realms we do know that I cannot believe it is mere dreamland.

It is a thing impossible to illustrate by short quotations, but I can point to passages where I have felt it in especial force. One comes in the last chapter of *All Hallows' Eve*, where Lester, who has been, in the physical sense, dead for many days, looks up and discovers (I cannot explain this without telling the whole story) that a still more final separation is at hand. Then come the words 'All, all was ending; this, after so many preludes, was certainly death. This was the most exquisite and pure joy of death. . . . Above her the sky every moment grew more high and empty; the rain fell from a source beyond all clouds.'

Another comes in the fourth chapter of the *Descent into Hell*, where the aged Margaret, on her death bed, feels herself to be at once a mountain and a traveller who climbs that mountain: and 'Now she knew that only the smallest fragility of her being clung somewhere to the great height that was she and others and all the world under her separate kind, as she herself was part of all the other peaks.' You may, of course, ask me how Williams should know. And I am not suggesting that he knows in one sense—that he is giving me factual details about the world beyond death or on the brink of death. What I am quite sure of is that he is describing something he knows which I should not have known unless he had described it; and something that matters.

But I am horribly afraid lest what I said earlier about his good characters should leave anyone under the impression that he was a moralist. The public has a distrust for moral books which is not wholly mistaken. Morality has spoiled literature often enough: we all remember what happened to some nineteenth-century novels. The truth is, it is very bad to reach the stage of thinking deeply and frequently about duty unless you are prepared to go a stage further. The Law, as St Paul first clearly explained, only takes you to the school gates. Morality exists to be transcended. We act from duty in the hope that someday we shall do the same acts freely and delightfully. It is one of the liberating qualities in Williams's books that we are hardly ever on the merely moral level.

One little fact is significant; the unexpected extension he gives to the idea of courtesy. What others would regard as service or unselfishness he regards as good manners. That, taken by itself, might be a mere verbal trick: I mention it here only as a convenient shorthand symbol for the whole attitude. For courtesy can be frolic or ceremonial—or both—where unselfishness is lumpish and portentous. And that sublimation of merely ethical attitudes is at work though all his writing. His world may be fierce and perilous; but the sense of grandeur, of exuberance, even of carnival, the *honestade* and *cavalleria*, are never lost. It is a little like Spinoza's *hilaritas*, if Spinoza could have progressed from his geometrical method to dance his philosophy. Even the chief fault of the earlier books—the perilous approach to flippancy in the dialogue—was a prentice attempt to express his own sense of gay adventure in the spiritual life. No doubt, some pious readers find Williams embarrassingly at ease in Sion: if so, have they forgotten that David danced before the Ark?

A Tribute to
E. R. Eddison

It is very rarely that a middle-aged man finds an author who gives him, what he knew so often in his teens and twenties, the sense of having opened a new door. One had thought those days were past. Eddison's heroic romances disproved it. Here was a new literary species, a new rhetoric, a new climate of the imagination. Its effect is not evanescent, for the whole life and strength of a singularly massive and consistent personality lies behind it. Still less, however, is it mere self-expression, appealing only to those whose subjectivity resembles the author's: admirers of Eddison differ in age and sex and include some (like myself) to whom his world is alien and even sinister. In a word, these books are works, first and foremost, of *art*. And they are irreplaceable. Nowhere else shall we meet this precise blend of hardness and luxury, of lawless speculation and sharply realised detail, of the cynical and the magnanimous. No author can be said to remind us of Eddison.

On Three Ways of Writing for Children

I think there are three ways in which those who write for children may approach their work; two good ways and one that is generally a bad way.

I came to know of the bad way quite recently and from two unconscious witnesses. One was a lady who sent me the MS of a story she had written in which a fairy placed at a child's disposal a wonderful gadget. I say 'gadget' because it was not a magic ring or hat or cloak or any such traditional matter. It was a machine, a thing of taps and handles and buttons you could press. You could press one and get an ice cream, another and get a live puppy, and so forth. I had to tell the author honestly that I didn't much care for that sort of thing. She replied 'No more do I, it bores me to distraction. But it is what the modern child wants.' My other bit of evidence was this. In my own first story I had described at length what I thought a rather fine high tea given by a hospitable faun to the little girl who was my heroine. A man, who has children of his own, said, 'Ah, I see how you got to that. If you want to please grown-up readers you give them sex, so you thought to yourself, "That won't do for children, what shall I give them instead? I know! The little blighters like plenty of good eating."' In reality, however, I myself like eating and drinking. I put in what I would have liked to read when I was a child and what I still like reading now that I am in my fifties.

The lady in my first example, and the married man in my

31

On Three Ways of Writing for Children

second, both conceived writing for children as a special depart-
ment of 'giving the public what it wants'. Children are, of course,
a special public and you find out what they want and give them
that, however little you like it yourself.

The next way may seem at first to be very much the same,
but I think the resemblance is superficial. This is the way of Lewis
Carroll, Kenneth Grahame, and Tolkien. The printed story grows
out of a story told to a particular child with the living voice and
perhaps *ex tempore*. It resembles the first way because you are
certainly trying to give that child what it wants. But then you are
dealing with a concrete person, this child who, of course, differs
from all other children. There is no question of 'children'
conceived as a strange species whose habits you have 'made up'
like an anthropologist or a commercial traveller. Nor, I suspect,
would it be possible, thus face to face, to regale the child with
things calculated to please it but regarded by yourself with
indifference or contempt. The child, I am certain, would see
through that. You would become slightly different because you
were talking to a child and the child would become slightly
different because it was being talked to by an adult. A com-
munity, a composite personality, is created and out of that the
story grows.

The third way, which is the only one I could ever use myself,
consists in writing a children's story because a children's story is
the best art-form for something you have to say: just as a
composer might write a Dead March not because there was a
public funeral in view but because certain musical ideas that had
occurred to him went best into that form. This method could
apply to other kinds of children's literature besides stories. I have
been told that Arthur Mee never met a child and never wished to:
it was, from his point of view, a bit of luck that boys liked reading
what he liked writing. This anecdote may be untrue in fact but it
illustrates my meaning.

Within the species 'children's story' the sub-species which
happened to suit me is the fantasy or (in a loose sense of that
word) the fairy tale. There are, of course, other sub-species.
E. Nesbit's trilogy about the Bastable family is a very good
specimen of another kind. It is a 'children's story' in the sense that

32

children can and do read it: but it is also the only form in which E. Nesbit could have given us so much of the humours of childhood. It is true that the Bastable children appear, successfully treated from the adult point of view, in one of her grownup novels, but they appear only for a moment. I do not think she would have kept it up. Sentimentality is so apt to creep in if we write at length about children as seen by their elders. And the reality of childhood, as we all experienced it, creeps out. For we all remember that our childhood, as lived, was immeasurably different from what our elders saw. Hence Sir Michael Sadler, when I asked his opinion about a certain new experimental school, replied, 'I never give an opinion on any of those experiments till the children have grown up and can tell us *what really happened.*' Thus, the Bastable trilogy, however improbable many of its episodes may be, provides even adults, in one sense, with more realistic reading about children than they could find in most books addressed to adults. But also, conversely, it enables the children who read it to do something much more mature than they realise. For the whole book is a character study of Oswald, an unconsciously satiric self-portrait, which every intelligent child can fully appreciate: but no child would sit down to read a character study in any other form. There is another way in which children's stories mediate this psychological interest, but I will reserve that for later treatment.

In this short glance at the Bastable trilogy I think we have stumbled on a principle. Where the children's story is simply the right form for what the author has to say, then of course readers who want to hear that will read the story or re-read it, at any age. I never met *The Wind in the Willows* or the Bastable books till I was in my late twenties, and I do not think I have enjoyed them any the less on that account. I am almost inclined to set it up as a canon that a children's story which is enjoyed only by children is a bad children's story. The good ones last. A waltz which you can like only when you are waltzing is a bad waltz.

This canon seems to me most obviously true of that particular type of children's story which is dearest to my own taste, the fantasy or fairy tale. Now the modern critical world uses 'adult' as a term of approval. It is hostile to what it calls 'nostalgia' and contemptuous of what it calls 'Peter Pantheism'. Hence a man who admits that dwarfs and giants and talking beasts and witches are still dear to him in his fifty-third year is now less likely to be praised for his perennial youth than scorned and pitied for arrested development. If I spend some little time defending myself against these charges, this is not so much because it matters greatly whether I am scorned and pitied as because the defence is germane to my whole view of the fairy tale and even of literature in general. My defence consists of three propositions.

1. I reply with a *tu quoque*. Critics who treat *adult* as a term of approval, instead of as a merely descriptive term, cannot be adult themselves. To be concerned about being grown up, to admire the grown up because it is grown up, to blush at the suspicion of being childish; these things are the marks of childhood and adolescence. And in childhood and adolescence they are, in moderation, healthy symptoms. Young things ought to want to grow. But to carry on into middle life or even into early manhood this concern about being adult is a mark of really arrested development. When I was ten, I read fairy tales in secret and would have been ashamed if I had been found doing so. Now that I am fifty I read them openly. When I became a man I put away childish things, including the fear of childishness and the desire to be very grown up.

2. The modern view seems to me to involve a false conception of growth. They accuse us of arrested development because we have not lost a taste we had in childhood. But surely arrested development consists not in refusing to lose old things but in failing to add new things? I now like hock, which I am sure I should not have liked as a child. But I still like lemon-squash. I call this growth or development because I have been enriched: where I formerly had only one pleasure, I now have two. But if I had to lose the taste for lemon-squash before I acquired the taste for hock, that would not be growth but simple change. I now enjoy Tolstoy and Jane Austen and Trollope as well as fairy tales and I call that growth: if I had had to lose the fairy tales in order to acquire the novelists, I would not say that I had grown but only that I had changed. A tree grows because it adds rings: a

train doesn't grow by leaving one station behind and puffing on to the next. In reality, the case is stronger and more complicated than this. I think my growth is just as apparent when I now read the fairy tales as when I read the novelists, for I now enjoy the fairy tales better than I did in childhood: being now able to put more in, of course I get more out. But I do not here stress that point. Even if it were merely a taste for grown-up literature added to an unchanged taste for children's literature, addition would still be entitled to the name 'growth', and the process of merely dropping one parcel when you pick up another would not. It is, of course, true that the process of growing does, incidentally and unfortunately, involve some more losses. But that is not the essence of growth, certainly not what makes growth admirable or desirable. If it were, if to drop parcels and to leave stations behind were the essence and virtue of growth, why should we stop at the adult? Why should not *senile* be equally a term of approval? Why are we not to be congratulated on losing our teeth and hair? Some critics seem to confuse growth with the cost of growth and also to wish to make that cost far higher than, in nature, it need be.

3. The whole association of fairy tale and fantasy with childhood is local and accidental. I hope everyone has read Tolkien's essay on Fairy Tales, which is perhaps the most important contribution to the subject that anyone has yet made. If so, you will know already that, in most places and times, the fairy tale has not been specially made for, nor exclusively enjoyed by, children. It has gravitated to the nursery when it became unfashionable in literary circles, just as unfashionable furniture gravitated to the nursery in Victorian houses. In fact, many children do not like this kind of book, just as many children do not like horsehair sofas: and many adults do like it, just as many adults like rocking chairs. And those who do like it, whether young or old, probably like it for the same reason. And none of us can say with any certainty what that reason is. The two theories which are most often in my mind are those of Tolkien and of Jung.

According to Tolkien* the appeal of the fairy story lies in the fact that man there most fully exercises his function as a

---

* 'On Fairy-Stories', *Essays Presented to Charles Williams* (1947).

'subcreator'; not, as they love to say now, making a 'comment upon life' but making, so far as possible, a subordinate world of his own. Since, in Tolkien's view, this is one of man's proper functions, delight naturally arises whenever it is successfully performed. For Jung, fairy tale liberates Archetypes which dwell in the collective unconscious, and when we read a good fairy tale we are obeying the old precept 'Know thyself'. I would venture to add to this my own theory, not indeed of the Kind as a whole, but of one feature in it: I mean, the presence of beings other than human which yet behave, in varying degrees, humanly: the giants and dwarfs and talking beasts. I believe these to be at least (for they may have many other sources of power and beauty) an admirable hieroglyphic which conveys psychology, types of character, more briefly than novelistic presentation and to readers whom novelistic presentation could not yet reach. Consider Mr Badger in *The Wind in the Willows*—that extraordinary amalgam of high rank, coarse manners, gruffness, shyness, and goodness. The child who has once met Mr Badger has ever afterwards, in its bones, a knowledge of humanity and of English social history which it could not get in any other way.

Of course as all children's literature is not fantastic, so all fantastic books need not be children's books. It is still possible, even in an age so ferociously anti-romantic as our own, to write fantastic stories for adults: though you will usually need to have made a name in some more fashionable kind of literature before anyone will publish them. But there may be an author who at a particular moment finds not only fantasy but fantasy-for-children the exactly right form for what he wants to say. The distinction is a fine one. His fantasies for children and his fantasies for adults will have very much more in common with one another than either has with the ordinary novel or with what is sometimes called 'the novel of child life'. Indeed the same readers will probably read both his fantastic 'juveniles' and his fantastic stories for adults. For I need not remind such an audience as this that the neat sorting-out of books into age-groups, so dear to publishers, has only a very sketchy relation with the habits of any real readers. Those of us who are blamed when old for reading childish books were blamed when children for reading books too old for us. No reader worth his salt trots along in obedience to a time-table. The distinction, then, is a fine one: and I am not quite sure what made me, in a particular year of my life, feel that not only a fairy tale, but a fairy tale addressed to children, was exactly what I must write—or burst. Partly, I think, that this form permits, or compels you to leave out things I wanted to leave out. It compels you to throw all the force of the book into what was done and said. It checks what a kind, but discerning critic called 'the expository demon' in me. It also imposes certain very fruitful necessities about length.

If I have allowed the fantastic type of children's story to run away with this discussion, that is because it is the kind I know and love best, not because I wish to condemn any other. But the patrons of the other kinds very frequently want to condemn it. About once every hundred years some wiseacre gets up and tries to banish the fairy tale. Perhaps I had better say a few words in its defence, as reading for children.

It is accused of giving children a false impression of the world they live in. But I think no literature that children could read gives them less of a false impression. I think what profess to be realistic stories for children are far more likely to deceive them. I never expected the real world to be like the fairy tales. I think that I did expect school to be like the school stories. The fantasies did not deceive me: the school stories did. All stories in which children have adventures and successes which are possible, in the sense that they do not break the laws of nature, but almost infinitely improbable, are in more danger than the fairy tales of raising false expectations.

Almost the same answer serves for the popular charge of escapism, though here the question is not so simple. Do fairy tales teach children to retreat into a world of wish-fulfilment— 'fantasy' in the technical psychological sense of the word—instead of facing the problems of the real world? Now it is here that the problem becomes subtle. Let us again lay the fairy tale side by side with the school story or any other story which is labelled a 'Boy's Book' or a 'Girl's Book', as distinct from a 'Children's Book'. There is no doubt that both arouse, and imaginatively satisfy, wishes. We long to go through the looking glass, to reach fairy land. We also long to be the immensely popular and successful schoolboy or schoolgirl, or the lucky boy or girl who discovers the spy's plot or rides the horse that none of the cowboys can manage. But the two longings are very different. The second, especially when directed on something so close as school life, is ravenous and deadly serious. Its fulfilment on the level of imagination is in very truth compensatory: we run to it from the disappointments and humiliations of the real world: it sends us back to the real world undivinely discontented. For it is all flattery to the ego. The pleasure consists in picturing oneself the object of admiration. The other longing, that for fairy land, is very different. In a sense a child does not long for fairy land as a boy longs to be the hero of the first eleven. Does anyone suppose that he really and prosaically longs for all the dangers and discomforts of a fairy tale?—really wants dragons in contemporary England? It is not so. It would be much truer to say that fairy land arouses a longing for he knows not what. It stirs and troubles him (to his life-long enrichment) with the dim sense of something beyond his reach and, far from dulling or emptying the actual world, gives it a new dimension of depth. He does not despise real woods because he has read of enchanted woods: the reading makes all real woods a little enchanted. This is a special kind of longing. The boy reading the school story of the type I have in mind desires success and is unhappy (once the book is over) because he can't get it: the boy reading the fairy tale desires and is happy in the very fact of desiring. For his mind has not been concentrated on himself, as it often is in the more realistic story.

I do not mean that school stories for boys and girls ought not to be written. I am only saying that they are far more liable to become 'fantasies' in the clinical sense than fantastic stories are. And this distinction holds for adult reading too. The dangerous fantasy is always superficially realistic. The real victim of wishful reverie does not batten on the *Odyssey, The Tempest,* or *The Worm Ouroboros*: he (or she) prefers stories about millionaires, irresistible beauties, posh hotels, palm beaches and bedroom scenes—things that really might happen, that ought to happen, that would have happened if the reader had had a fair chance. For, as I say, there are two kinds of longing. The one is an *askesis*, a spiritual exercise, and the other is a disease.

A far more serious attack on the fairy tale as children's literature comes from those who do not wish children to be frightened. I suffered too much from night-fears myself in childhood to undervalue this objection. I would not wish to heat the fires of that private hell for any child. On the other hand, none of my fears came from fairy tales. Giant insects were my speciality, with ghosts a bad second. I suppose the ghosts came directly or indirectly from stories, though certainly not from fairy stories, but I don't think the insects did. I don't know anything my parents could have done or left undone which would have saved me from the pincers, mandibles, and eyes of those many-legged abominations. And that, as so many people have pointed out, is the difficulty. We do not know what will or will not frighten a child in this particular way. I say 'in this particular way' for we must here make a distinction. Those who say that children must not be frightened may mean two things. They may mean (1) that we must not do anything likely to give the child those haunting, disabling, pathological fears against which ordinary courage is helpless: in fact, *phobias*. His mind must, if possible, be kept clear of things he can't bear to think of. Or they may mean (2) that we must try to keep out of his mind the knowledge that he is born into a world of death, violence, wounds, adventure, heroism and cowardice, good and evil. If they mean the first I agree with them: but not if they mean the second. The second would indeed be to give children a false impression and feed them on escapism in the bad sense. There is something ludicrous in the idea of so educating a generation which is born to the Ogpu and the atomic bomb. Since it is so likely that they will meet cruel enemies, let them at least have heard of brave knights and heroic courage. Otherwise you are making their destiny not brighter but darker. Nor do most of us find that violence and bloodshed, in a story, produce any haunting dread in the minds of children. As far as that goes, I side impenitently with the human race against the modern reformer. Let there be wicked kings and beheadings, battles and dungeons, giants and dragons, and let villains be soundly killed at the end of the book. Nothing will persuade me that this causes an ordinary child any kind or degree of fear beyond what it wants, and needs, to feel. For, of course, it wants to be a little frightened.

The other fears—the phobias—are a different matter. I do not believe one can control them by literary means. We seem to bring them into the world with us ready made. No doubt the particular image on which the child's terror is fixed can sometimes be traced to a book. But is that the source, or only the occasion, of the fear? If he had been spared that image, would not some other, quite unpredictable by you, have had the same effect? Chesterton has told us of a boy who was more afraid of the Albert Memorial than anything else in the world. I know a man whose great childhood terror was the India paper edition of the *Encyclopaedia Britannica*— for a reason I defy you to guess. And I think it possible that by confining your child to blameless stories of child life in which nothing at all alarming ever happens, you would fail to banish the terrors, and would succeed in banishing all that can ennoble them or make them endurable. For in the fairy tales, side by side with the terrible figures, we find the immemorial comforters and protectors, the radiant ones; and the terrible figures are not merely terrible, but sublime. It would be nice if no little boy in bed, hearing, or thinking he hears, a sound, were ever at all frightened. But if he is going to be frightened, I think it better that he should think of giants and dragons than merely of burglars. And I think St George, or any bright champion in armour, is a better comfort than the idea of the police.

I will even go further. If I could have escaped all my own night-fears at the price of never having known 'faerie', would I now be the gainer by that bargain? I am not speaking carelessly. The fears were very bad. But I think the price would have been too high.

But I have strayed far from my theme. This has been inevitable for, of the three methods, I know by experience only the third. I hope my title did not lead anyone to think that I was conceited enough to give you advice on how to write a story for children. There were two very good reasons for not doing that. One is that many people have written very much better stories than I, and I would rather learn about the art than set up to teach it. The other is that, in a certain sense, I have never exactly 'made' a story. With me the process is much more like bird-watching than like either talking or building. I see pictures. Some of these pictures have a common flavour, almost a common smell, which groups them together. Keep quiet and watch and they will begin joining themselves up. If you were very lucky (I have never been as lucky as all that) a whole set might join themselves so consistently that there you had a complete story; without doing anything yourself. But more often (in my experience always) there are gaps. Then at last you have to do some deliberate inventing, have to contrive reasons why these characters should be in these various places doing these various things. I have no idea whether this is the usual way of writing stories, still less whether it is the best. It is the only one I know: images always come first.

Before closing, I would like to return to what I said at the beginning. I rejected any approach which begins with the question 'What do modern children like?' I might be asked, 'Do you equally reject the approach which begins with the question "What do modern children need?"'—in other words, with the moral or didactic approach?' I think the answer is Yes. Not because I don't like stories to have a moral: certainly not because I think children dislike a moral. Rather because I feel sure that the question 'What do modern children need?' will not lead you to a good moral. If we ask that question we are assuming too superior an attitude. It would be better to ask 'What moral do I need?' for I think we can be sure that what does not concern us deeply will not deeply interest our readers, whatever their age. But it is better not to ask the questions at all. Let the pictures tell you their own moral. For the moral inherent in them will rise from whatever spiritual roots you have succeeded in striking during the whole course of your life. But if they don't show you any moral, don't put one in. For the moral you put in is likely to be a platitude, or even a falsehood, skimmed from the surface of your consciousness. It is impertinent to offer the children that. For we have been told on high authority that in the moral sphere they are probably at least as wise as we. Anyone who *can* write a children's story without a moral, had better do so: that is, if he is going to write children's stories at all. The only moral that is of any value is that which arises inevitably from the whole cast of the author's mind.

Indeed everything in the story should arise from the whole cast of the author's mind. We must write for children out of those elements in our own imagination which we share with children; differing from our child readers not by any less, or less serious, interest in the things we handle, but by the fact that we have other interests which children would not share with us. The matter of our story should be a part of the habitual furniture of our minds. This, I fancy, has been so with all great writers for children, but it is not generally understood. A critic not long ago said in praise of a very serious fairy tale that the author's tongue 'never once got into his cheek'. But why on earth should it?— unless he had been eating a seed-cake. Nothing seems to me more fatal, for this art, than an idea that whatever we share with children is, in the privative sense, 'childish' and that whatever is childish is somehow comic. We must meet children as equals in that area of our nature where we are their equals. Our superiority consists partly in commanding other areas, and partly (which is more relevant) in the fact that we are better at telling stories than they are. The child as reader is neither to be patronised nor idolised: we talk to him as man to man. But the worst attitude of all would be the professional attitude which regards children in the lump as a sort of raw material which we have to handle. We must of course try to do them no harm: we may, under the Omnipotence, sometimes dare to hope that we may do them good. But only such good as involves treating them with respect. We must not imagine that we are Providence or Destiny. I will not say that a good story for children could never be written by someone in the Ministry of Education, for all things are possible. But I should lay very long odds against it.

Once in a hotel dining-room I said, rather too loudly, 'I loathe prunes.' 'So do I,' came an unexpected six-year-old voice from another table. Sympathy was instantaneous. Neither of us thought it funny. We both knew that prunes are far too nasty to be funny. That is the proper meeting between man and child as independent personalities. Of the far higher and more difficult relations beween child and parent or child and teacher, I say nothing. An author, as a mere author, is outside all that. He is not even an uncle. He is a freeman and an equal, like the postman, the butcher, and the dog next door.

Sometimes Fairy Stories May Say Best What's to Be Said

In the sixteenth century when everyone was saying that poets (by which they meant all imaginative writers) ought 'to please and instruct', Tasso made a valuable distinction. He said that the poet, as poet, was concerned solely with pleasing. But then every poet was also a man and a citizen; in that capacity he ought to, and would wish to, make his work edifying as well as pleasing.

Now I do not want to stick very close to the renaissance ideas of 'pleasing' and 'instructing'. Before I could accept either term it might need so much redefining that what was left of it at the end would not be worth retaining. All I want to use is the distinction between the author as author and the author as man, citizen, or Christian. What this comes to for me is that there are usually two reasons for writing an imaginative work, which may be called Author's reason and the Man's. If only one of these is present, then, so far as I am concerned, the book will not be written. If the first is lacking, it can't; if the second is lacking, it shouldn't.

In the Author's mind there bubbles up every now and then the material for a story. For me it invariably begins with mental pictures. This ferment leads to nothing unless it is accompanied with the longing for a Form: verse or prose, short story, novel, play or what not. When these two things click you have the Author's impulse complete. It is now a thing inside him pawing to get out. He longs to see that bubbling stuff pouring into that Form as the housewife longs to see the new jam pouring into the clean jam jar. This nags him all day long and gets in the way of his work and his sleep and his meals. It's like being in love.

While the Author is in this state, the Man will of course have to criticise the proposed book from quite a different point of view. He will ask how the gratification of this impulse will fit in with all the other things he wants, and ought to do or be. Perhaps the whole thing is too frivolous and trivial (from the Man's point of view, not the Author's) to justify the time and pains it would involve. Perhaps it would be unedifying when it was done. Or else perhaps (at this point the Author cheers up) it looks like being 'good', not in a merely literary sense, but 'good' all around.

This may sound rather complicated but it is really very like what happens about other things. You are attracted by a girl; but is she the sort of girl you'd be wise, or right, to marry? You would like to have lobster for lunch; but does it agree with you and is it wicked to spend that amount of money on a meal? The Author's impulse is a desire (it is very like an itch), and of course, like every other desire, needs to be criticised by the whole Man.

Let me now apply this to my own fairy tales. Some people seem to think that I began by asking myself how I could say something about Christianity to children; then fixed on the fairy tale as an instrument; then collected information about child-psychology and decided what age-group I'd write for; then drew up a list of basic Christian truths and hammered out 'allegories' to embody them. This is all pure moonshine. I couldn't write in that way at all. Everything began with images; a faun carrying an umbrella, a queen on a sledge, a magnificent lion. At first there wasn't even anything Christian about them; that element pushed itself in of its own accord. It was part of the bubbling.

Then came the Form. As these images sorted themselves into events (i.e., became a story) they seemed to demand no love interest and no close psychology. But the Form which excludes these things is the fairy tale. And the moment I thought of that I fell in love with the Form itself: its brevity, its severe restraints on description, its flexible traditionalism, its inflexible hostility to all analysis, digression, reflections and 'gas'. I was now enamoured of it. Its very limitations of vocabulary became an attraction; as the hardness of the stone pleases the sculptor or the difficulty of the sonnet delights the sonneteer.

On that side (as Author) I wrote fairy tales because the Fairy Tale seemed the ideal Form for the stuff I had to say.

Then of course the Man in me began to have his turn. I thought I saw how stories of this kind could steal past a certain inhibition which had paralysed much of my own religion in childhood. Why did one find it so hard to feel as one was told one ought to feel about God or about the sufferings of Christ? I thought the chief reason was that one was told one ought to. An obligation to feel can freeze feelings. And reverence itself did harm. The whole subject was associated with lowered voices; almost as if it were something medical. But supposing that by casting all these things into an imaginary world, stripping them of their stained-glass and Sunday school associations, one could make them for the first time appear in their real potency? Could one not thus steal past those watchful dragons? I thought one could.

That was the Man's motive. But of course he could have done nothing if the Author had not been on the boil first.

You will notice that I have throughout spoken of Fairy Tales, not 'children's stories'. Professor J. R. R. Tolkien in *The Lord of the Rings** has shown that the connection between fairy tales and children is not nearly so close as publishers and educationalists think. Many children don't like them and many adults do. The truth is, as he says, that they are now associated with children because they are out of fashion with adults; have in fact retired to the nursery as old furniture used to retire there, not because the children had begun to like it but because their elders had ceased to like it.

I was therefore writing 'for children' only in the sense that I excluded what I thought they would not like or understand; not in the sense of writing what I intended to be below adult attention. I may of course have been deceived, but the principle at

---

*I think Lewis really meant Professor Tolkien's essay 'On Fairy-Stories' in *Essays Presented to Charles Williams*.

least saves one from being patronising. I never wrote down to anyone; and whether the opinion condemns or acquits my own work, it certainly is my opinion that a book worth reading only in childhood is not worth reading even then. The inhibitions which I hoped my stories would overcome in a child's mind may exist in a grown-up's mind too, and may perhaps be overcome by the same means.

The Fantastic or Mythical is a Mode available at all ages for some readers; for others, at none. At all ages, if it is well used by the author and meets the right reader, it has the same power: to generalise while remaining concrete, to present in palpable form not concepts or even experiences but whole classes of experience, and to throw off irrelevancies. But at its best it can do more; it can give us experiences we have never had and thus, instead of 'commenting on life', can add to it. I am speaking, of course, about the thing itself, not my own attempts at it.

'Juveniles', indeed! Am I to patronise sleep because children sleep sound? Or honey because children like it?

On
Juvenile Tastes

Not long ago I saw in some periodical the statement that 'Children are a distinct race'. Something like this seems to be assumed today by many who write, and still more who criticise, what are called children's books or 'juveniles'. Children are regarded as being at any rate a distinct *literary* species, and the production of books that cater for their supposedly odd and alien taste has become an industry; almost a heavy one.

This theory does not seem to me to be borne out by the facts. For one thing, there is no literary taste common to all children. We find among them all the same types as among ourselves. Many of them, like many of us, never read when they can find any other entertainment. Some of them choose quiet, realistic, 'slice-of-life' books (say, *The Daisy Chain*), as some of us choose Trollope.

Some like fantasies and marvels, as some of us like the *Odyssey*, Boiardo, Ariosto, Spenser, or Mr Mervyn Peake. Some care for little but books of information, and so do some adults. Some of them, like some of us, are omnivorous. Silly children prefer success stories about school life as silly adults like success stories about grown-up life.

We can approach the matter in a different way by drawing up a list of books which, I am told, have been generally liked by the young. I suppose Aesop, *The Arabian Nights, Gulliver, Robinson Crusoe, Treasure Island, Peter Rabbit,* and *The Wind in the Willows* would be a reasonable choice. Only the last three were written for

49

children, and those three are read with pleasure by many adults. I, who disliked *The Arabian Nights* as a child, dislike them still.

It may be argued against this that the enjoyment by children of some books intended for their elders does not in the least refute the doctrine that there is a specifically childish taste. They select (you may say) that minority of ordinary books which happens to suit them, as a foreigner in England may select those English dishes which come nearest to suiting his alien palate. And the specifically childish taste has been generally held to be that for the adventurous and the marvellous.

Now this, you may notice, implies that we are regarding as specifically childish a taste which in many, perhaps in most, times and places has been that of the whole human race. Those stories from Greek or Norse mythology, from Homer, from Spenser, or from folklore which children (but by no means all children) read with delight were once the delight of everyone.

Even the fairy tale *proprement dit* was not originally intended for children; it was told and enjoyed in (of all places) the court of Louis XIV. As Professor Tolkien has pointed out, it gravitated to the nursery when it went out of fashion among the grown-ups, just as old-fashioned furniture gravitated to the nursery. Even if all children and no adults now liked the marvellous—and neither is the case—we ought not to say that the peculiarity of children lies in their liking it. The peculiarity is that they *still* like it, even in the twentieth century.

It does not seem to me useful to say, 'What delighted the infancy of the species naturally still delights the infancy of the individual'. This involves a parallel between individual and species which we are in no position to draw. What age is Man? Is the race now in its childhood, its maturity, or its dotage? As we don't know at all exactly when it began, and have no notion when it will end, this seems a nonsense question. And who knows if it will ever be mature? Man may be killed in infancy.

Surely it would be less arrogant, and truer to the evidence, to say that the peculiarity of child readers is that they are not peculiar. It is we who are peculiar. Fashions in literary taste come and go among the adults, and every period has its own shibboleths. These, when good, do not improve the taste of children, and, when bad, do not corrupt it; for children read only to enjoy. Of course their limited vocabulary and general ignorance make some books unintelligible to them. But apart from that, juvenile taste is simply human taste, going on from age to age, silly with a universal silliness or wise with a universal wisdom, regardless of modes, movements, and literary revolutions.

This has one curious result. When the literary Establishment—the approved canon of taste—is so extremely jejune and narrow as it is today, much has to be addressed in the first instance to children if it is to get printed at all. Those who have a story to tell must appeal to the audience that still cares for story-telling.

The literary world of today is little interested in the narrative art as such; it is preoccupied with technical novelties and with 'ideas', by which it means not literary, but social or psychological, ideas. The ideas (in the literary sense) on which Miss Norton's *The Borrowers* or Mr White's *Mistress Masham's Response* are built would not need to be embodied in 'juveniles' at most periods.

It follows that there are now two very different sorts of 'writers for children'. The wrong sort believe that children are 'a distinct race'. They carefully 'make up' the tastes of these odd creatures—like an anthropologist observing the habits of a savage tribe—or even the tastes of a clearly defined age-group within a particular social class within the 'distinct race'. They dish up not what they like themselves but what that race is supposed to like. Educational and moral, as well as commercial, motives may come in.

The right sort work from the common, universally human, ground they share with the children, and indeed with countless adults. They label their books 'For Children' because children are the only market now recognised for the books they, anyway, want to write.

It All Began
with a Picture ...

The Editor has asked me to tell you how I came to write *The Lion, the Witch and the Wardrobe*. I will try, but you must not believe all that authors tell you about how they wrote their books. This is not because they mean to tell lies. It is because a man writing a story is too excited about the story itself to sit back and notice how he is doing it. In fact, that might stop the works; just as, if you start thinking about how you tie your tie, the next thing is that you find you can't tie it. And afterwards, when the story is finished, he has forgotten a good deal of what writing it was like.

One thing I am sure of. All my seven Narnian books, and my three science-fiction books, began with seeing pictures in my head. At first they were not a story, just pictures. The *Lion* all began with a picture of a Faun carrying an umbrella and parcels in a snowy wood. This picture had been in my mind since I was about sixteen. Then one day, when I was about forty, I said to myself: 'Let's try to make a story about it'.

At first I had very little idea how the story would go. But then suddenly Aslan came bounding into it. I think I had been having a good many dreams of lions about that time. Apart from that, I don't know where the Lion came from or why He came. But once He was there He pulled the whole story together, and soon He pulled the six other Narnian stories in after Him.

So you see that, in a sense, I know very little about how this story was born. That is, I don't know where the pictures came from. And I don't believe anyone knows exactly how he 'makes things up'. Making up is a very mysterious thing. When you 'have an idea' could you tell anyone exactly *how* you thought of it?

On
Science Fiction

Sometimes a village or small town which we have known all our lives becomes the scene of a murder, a novel, or a centenary, and then for a few months everyone knows its name and crowds go to visit it. A like thing happens to one's private recreations. I had been walking, and reading Trollope, for years when I found myself suddenly overtaken, as if by a wave from behind, by a boom in Trollope and a short-lived craze for what was called hiking. And lately I have had the same sort of experience again. I had read fantastic fiction of all sorts ever since I could read, including, of course, the particular kind which Wells practised in his *Time Machine, First Men in the Moon,* and others. Then, some fifteen or twenty years ago, I became aware of a bulge in the production of such stories. In America whole magazines began to be exclusively devoted to them. The execution was usually detestable; the conceptions, sometimes worthy of better treatment. About this time the name *scientifiction,* soon altered to *science fiction,* began to be common. Then, perhaps five or six years ago, the bulge still continuing and even increasing, there was an improvement: not that very bad stories cease to be the majority, but that the good ones became better and more numerous. It was after this that the genre began to attract the attention (always, I think, contemptuous) of the literary weeklies. There seems, in fact, to be a double paradox in its history: it began to be popular when it least deserved popularity, and to excite critical contempt as soon as it ceased to be wholly contemptible.

Of articles I have read on the subject (and I expect I have missed many) I do not find that I can make any use. For one thing, most were not very well informed. For another, many were by people who clearly hated the kind they wrote about. It is very dangerous to write about a kind you hate. Hatred obscures all distinctions. I don't like detective stories and therefore all detective stories look much alike to me: if I wrote about them I should therefore infallibly write drivel. Criticism of kinds, as distinct from criticism of works, cannot of course be avoided: I shall be driven to criticise one sub-species of science fiction myself. But it is, I think, the most subjective and least reliable type of criticism. Above all, it should not masquerade as criticism of individual works. Many reviews are useless because, while purporting to condemn the book, they only reveal the reviewer's dislike of the kind to which it belongs. Let bad tragedies be censured by those who love tragedy, and bad detective stories by those who love the detective story. Then we shall learn their real faults. Otherwise we shall find epics blamed for not being novels, farces for not being high comedies, novels by James for lacking the swift action of Smollett. Who wants to hear a particular claret abused by a fanatical teetotaller, or a particular woman by a confirmed misogynist?

Moreover, most of these articles were chiefly concerned to account for the bulge in the output and consumption of science fiction on sociological and psychological grounds. This is of course a perfectly legitimate attempt. But here as elsewhere those who hate the thing they are trying to explain are not perhaps those most likely to explain it. If you have never enjoyed a thing and do not know what it feels like to enjoy it, you will hardly know what sort of people go to it, in what moods, seeking what sort of gratification. And if you do not know what sort of people they are, you will be ill-equipped to find out what conditions have made them so. In this way, one may say of a kind not only (as Wordsworth says of the poet) that 'you must love it ere to you it will seem worthy of your love', but that you must at least have loved it once if you are even to warn others against it. Even if it is a vice to read science fiction, those who cannot understand the very temptation to that vice will not be likely to tell us anything of value about it. Just as I, for instance, who have no taste for cards, could not find anything very useful to say by way of warning against deep play. They will be like the frigid preaching chastity, misers warning us against prodigality, cowards denouncing rashness. And because, as I have said, hatred assimilates all the hated objects, it will make you assume that all the things lumped together as science fiction are of the same sort, and that the psychology of all those who like to read any of them is the same. That is likely to make the problem of explaining the bulge seem simpler than it really is.

I myself shall not attempt to explain it at all. I am not interested in the bulge. It is nothing to me whether a given work makes part of it or was written long before it occurred. The existence of the bulge cannot make the kind (or kinds) intrinsically better or worse; though of course bad specimens will occur most often within it.

I will now try to divide this species of narrative into its sub-species. I shall begin with that sub-species which I think radically bad, in order to get it out of our way.

In this sb-species the author leaps forward into an imagined future when planetary, sidereal, or even galactic travel has become common. Against this huge backcloth he then proceeds to develop an ordinary love-story, spy-story, wreck-story, or crime-story. This seems to me tasteless. Whatever in a work of art is not used is doing harm. The faintly imagined, and sometimes strictly unimaginable, scene and properties, only blur the real theme and distract us from any interest it might have had. I presume that the authors of such stories are, so to speak, Displaced Persons— commercial authors who did not really want to write science fiction at all, but who availed themselves of its popularity by giving a veneer of science fiction to their normal kind of work. But we must distinguish. A leap into the future, a rapid assumption of all the changes which are feigned to have occurred, is a legitimate 'machine' if it enables the author to develop a story of real value which could not have been told (or not so economically) in any other way. Thus John Collier in *Tom's A-Cold*

(1933) wants to write a story of heroic action among people themselves semi-barbarous but supported by the surviving tradition of a literate culture recently overthrown. He could, of course, find an historical situation suitable to his purpose, somewhere in the early Dark Ages. But that would involve all manner of archæological details which would spoil his book if they were done perfunctorily and perhaps distract our interest if they were done well. He is therefore, on my view, fully justified in positing such a state of affairs in England after the destruction of our present civilisation. That enables him (and us) to assume a familiar climate, flora, and fauna. He is not interested in the process whereby the change came about. That is all over before the curtain rises. This supposition is equivalent to the rules of his game; criticism applies only to the quality of his play. A much more frequent use of the leap into the future, in our time, is satiric or prophetic: the author criticises tendencies in the present by imagining them carried out ('produced', as Euclid would say) to their logical limit. *Brave New World* and *Nineteen Eighty-Four* leap to our minds. I can see no objection to such a 'machine'. Nor do I see much use in discussing, as someone did, whether books that use it can be called 'novels' or not. That is merely a question of definition. You may define the novel either so as to exclude or so as to include them. The best definition is that which proves itself most convenient. And of course to devise a definition for the purpose of excluding either *The Waves* in one direction or *Brave New World* in another, and then blame them for being excluded, is foolery.

I am, then, condemning not all books which suppose a future widely different from the present, but those which do so without a good reason, which leap a thousand years to find plots and passions which they could have found at home.

Having condemned that sub-species, I am glad to turn to another which I believe to be legitimate, though I have not the slightest taste for it myself. If the former is the fiction of the Displaced Persons, this might be called the fiction of Engineers. It is written by people who are primarily interested in space-travel, or in other undiscovered techniques, as real possibilities in the actual universe. They give us in imaginative form their guesses as to how the thing might be done. Jules Verne's *Twenty Thousand Leagues Under the Sea* and Wells's *Land Ironclads* were once specimens of this kind, though the coming of the real submarine and the real tank has altered their original interest. Arthur Clarke's *Prelude to Space* is another. I am too uneducated scientifically to criticise such stories on the mechanical side; and I am so completely out of sympathy with the projects they anticipate that I am incapable of criticising them as stories. I am as blind to their appeal as a pacifist is to *Maldon* and *Lepanto*, or an aristocratophobe (if I may coin the word) to the *Arcadia*. But heaven forbid that I should regard the limitations of my sympathy as anything save a red light which warns me not to criticise at all. For all I know, these may be very good stories in their own kind.

I think it useful to distinguish from these Engineers' Stories a third sub-species where the interest is, in a sense, scientific, but speculative. When we learn from the sciences the probable nature of places or conditions which no human being has experienced, there is, in normal men, an impulse to attempt to imagine them. Is any man such a dull clod that he can look at the moon through a good telescope without asking himself what it would be like to walk among those mountains under that black, crowded sky? The scientists themselves, the moment they go beyond purely mathematical statements, can hardly avoid describing the facts in terms of their probable effect on the senses of a human observer. Prolong this, and give, along with that observer's sense experience, his probable emotions and thoughts, and you at once have a rudimentary science fiction. And of course men have been doing this for centuries. What would Hades be like if you could go there alive? Homer sends Odysseus there and gives his answer. Or again, what would it be like at the Antipodes? (For this was a question of the same sort so long as men believed that the torrid zone rendered them forever inaccessible.) Dante takes you there: he describes with all the gusto of the later scientifictionist how surprising it was to see the sun in such an position. Better still, what would it be like if you could get to the centre of the earth? Dante tells you at the end of the *Inferno* where he and Virgil, after climbing down from the shoulders to the waist of Lucifer, find that they have to climb up from his waist to his feet, because of course they have passed the centre of gravitation. It is a perfect science-fiction effect. Thus again Athanasius Kircher in his *Iter Extaticum Celeste* (1656) will take you to all the planets and most of the stars, presenting as vividly as he can what you would see and feel if this were possible. He, like Dante, uses supernatural means of transport. In Wells's *First Men in the Moon* we have means which are feigned to be natural. What keeps his story within this sub-species, and distinguishes it from those of the Engineers, is his choice of a quite impossible composition called cavorite. This impossibility is of course a merit, not a defect. A man of his ingenuity could easily have thought up something more plausible. But the more plausible, the worse. That would merely invite interest in possibilities of reaching the Moon, an interest foreign to his story. Never mind how they got there; we are imagining what it would be like. The first glimpse of the unveiled airless sky, the lunar landscape, the lunar levity, the incomparable solitude, then the growing terror, finally the overwhelming approach of the lunar night—it is for these things that the story (especially in its original and shorter form) exists.

How anyone can think this form illegitimate or contemptible passes my understanding. It may very well be convenient not to call such things novels. If you prefer, call them a very special form of novels. Either way, the conclusion will be much the same: they are to be tried by their own rules. It is absurd to condemn them because they do not often display any deep or sensitive characterisation. They oughtn't to. It is a fault if they do. Wells's Cavor and Bedford have rather too much than too little character. Every good writer knows that the more unusual the scenes and events of his story are, the slighter, the more ordinary, the more typical his persons should be. Hence Gulliver is a commonplace little man and Alice a commonplace little girl. If they had been more remarkable they would have wrecked their books. The Ancient Mariner himself is a very ordinary man. To tell how odd things struck odd people is to have an oddity too much: he who is to see strange sights must not himself be strange. He ought to be as nearly as possible Everyman or Anyman. Of course, we must not confuse slight or typical characterisation with impossible or unconvincing characterisation. Falsification of character will always spoil a story. But character can apparently be reduced, simplified, to almost any extent with wholly satisfactory results. The greater ballads are an instance.

Of course, a given reader may be (some readers seem to be) interested in nothing else in the world except detailed studies of complex human personalities. If so, he has a good reason for not reading those kinds of work which neither demand nor admit it. He has no reason for condemning them, and indeed no qualification for speaking of them at all. We must not allow the novel of manners to give laws to all literature: let it rule its own domain. We must not listen to Pope's maxim about the proper study of mankind. The proper study of man is everything. The proper study of man as artist is everything which gives a foothold to the imagination and the passions.

But while I think this sort of science fiction legitimate, and capable of great virtues, it is not a kind which can endure copious production. It is only the first visit to the Moon or to Mars that is, for this purpose, any good. After each has been discovered in one or two stories (and turned out to be different in each) it becomes difficult to suspend our disbelief in favour of subsequent stories. However good they were they would kill each other by becoming numerous.

My next sub-species is what I would call the Eschatological. It is about the future, but not in the same way as *Brave New World* or *The Sleeper Awakes*. They were political or social. This kind gives an imaginative vehicle to speculations about the ultimate destiny of our species. Examples are Wells's *Time Machine*, Olaf Stapledon's *Last and First Men*, or Arthur Clarke's *Childhood's End*. It is here that a definition of science fiction which separates it entirely from the novel becomes imperative. The form of *Last and First Men* is not novelistic at all. It is indeed in a new form—the pseudo history. The pace, the concern with broad, general movements, the tone, are all those of the historiographer, not the novelist. It was the right form for the theme. And since we are here diverging so widely from the novel, I myself would gladly include in this sub-species a work which is not even narrative, Geoffrey Dennis's *The End of the World* (1930). And I would

certainly include, from J. B. S. Haldane's *Possible Worlds* (1927),
the brilliant, though to my mind depraved, paper called 'The
Last Judgement'.

Work of this kind gives expression to thoughts and emotions
which I think it good that we should sometimes entertain. It is
sobering and cathartic to remember, now and then, our collective
smallness, our apparent isolation, the apparent indifference of
nature, the slow biological, geological, and astronomical pro-
cesses which may, in the long run, make many of our hopes
(possibly some of our fears) ridiculous. If *memento mori* is sauce for
the individual, I do not know why the species should be spared
the taste of it. Stories of this kind may explain the hardly
disguised political rancour which I thought I detected in one
article on science fiction. The insinuation was that those who read
or wrote it were probably Fascists. What lurks behind such a hint
is, I suppose, something like this. If we were all on board ship
and there was trouble among the stewards, I can just conceive
their chief spokesman looking with disfavour on anyone who stole
away from the fierce debates in the saloon or pantry to take a
breather on deck. For up there, he would taste the salt, he would
see the vastness of the water, he would remember that the ship
had a whither and a whence. He would remember things like fog,
storms, and ice. What had seemed, in the hot, lighted rooms
down below to be merely the scene for a political crisis, would
appear once more as a tiny egg-shell moving rapidly through an
immense darkness over an element in which man cannot live. It
would not necessarily change his convictions about the rights and
wrongs of the dispute down below, but it would probably show
them in a new light. It could hardly fail to remind him that the
stewards were taking for granted hopes more momentous than
that of a rise in pay, and the passengers forgetting dangers more
serious than that of having to cook and serve their own meals.
Stories of the sort I am describing are like that visit to the deck.
They cool us. They are as refreshing as that passage in E. M.
Forster where the man, looking at the monkeys, realises that most
of the inhabitants of India do not care how India is governed.
Hence the uneasiness which they arouse in those who, for
whatever reason, wish to keep us wholly imprisoned in the

immediate conflict. That perhaps is why people are so ready with the charge of 'escape'. I never fully understood it till my friend Professor Tolkien asked me the very simple question, 'What class of men would you expect to be most preoccupied with, and most hostile to, the idea of escape?' and gave the obvious answer: jailers. The charge of Fascism is, to be sure, mere mud-flinging. Fascists, as well as Communists, are jailers; both would assure us that the proper study of prisoners is prison. But there is perhaps this truth behind it: that those who brood much on the remote past or future, or stare long at the night sky, are less likely than others to be ardent or orthodox partisans.

I turn at last to that sub-species in which alone I myself am greatly interested. It is best approached by reminding ourselves of a fact which every writer on the subject whom I have read completely ignores. Far the best of the American magazines bears the significant title *Fantasy and Science Fiction*. In it (as also in many other publications of the same type) you will find not only stories about space-travel but stories about gods, ghosts, ghouls, demons, fairies, monsters, etc. This gives us our clue. The last sub-species of science fiction represents simply an imaginative impulse as old as the human race working under the special conditions of our own time. It is not difficult to see why those who wish to visit strange regions in search of such beauty, awe, or terror as the actual world does not supply have increasingly been driven to other planets or other stars. It is the result of increasing geographical knowledge. The less known the real world is, the more plausibly your marvels can be located near at hand. As the area of knowledge spreads, you need to go further afield: like a man moving his house further and further out into the country as the new building estates catch him up. Thus in Grimm's *Märchen*, stories told by peasants in wooded country, you need only walk an hour's journey into the next forest to find a home for your witch or ogre. The author of *Beowulf* can put Grendel's lair in a place of which he himself says *Nis paet feor heonon Mil-gemearces*. Homer, writing for a maritime people has to take Odysseus several days' journey by sea before he meets Circe, Calypso, the Cyclops, or the Sirens. Old Irish has a form called the *immram*, a voyage among islands. Arthurian romance, oddly at first sight, seems usually content with the old *Märchen* machine of a neighbouring forest. Chrétien and his successors knew a great deal of real geography. Perhaps the explanation is that these romances are chiefly written by Frenchmen about Britain, and Britain in the past. *Huon of Bordeaux* places Oberon in the East. Spenser invents a country not in our universe at all; Sidney goes to an imaginary past in Greece. By the eighteeenth century we have to move well out into the country. Paltock and Swift take us to remote seas, Voltaire to America. Rider Haggard had to go to unexplored Africa or Tibet; Bulwer-Lytton, to the depths of the Earth. It might have been predicted that stories of this kind would, sooner or later, have to leave Tellus altogether. We know now that where Haggard put She and Kôr we should really find groundnut schemes or Mau Mau.

In this kind of story the pseudo-scientific apparatus is to be taken simply as a 'machine' in the sense which that word bore for the Neo-Classical critics. The most superficial appearance of plausibility—the merest sop to our critical intellect—will do. I am inclined to think that frankly supernatural methods are best. I took a hero once to Mars in a space-ship, but when I knew better I had angels convey him to Venus. Nor need the strange worlds, when we get there, be at all strictly tied to scientific probabilities. It is their wonder, or beauty, or suggestiveness that matters. When I myself put canals on Mars I believe I already knew that better telescopes had dissipated that old optical delusion. The point was that they were part of the Martian myth as it already existed in the common mind.

The defence and analysis of this kind are, accordingly, no different from those of fantastic or mythopoeic literature in general. But here sub-species and sub-sub-species break out in baffling multitude. The impossible—or things so immensely improbable that they have, imaginatively, the same status as the impossible—can be used in literature for many different purposes. I cannot hope to do more than suggest a few main types: the subject still awaits its Aristotle.

It may represent the intellect, almost completely free from emotion, at play. The purest specimen would be Abbott's *Flatland*, though even here some emotion arises from the sense (which it inculcates) of our own limitations—the consciousness that our own human awareness of the world is arbitrary and contingent. Sometimes such play gives a pleasure analogous to that of the conceit. I have unluckily forgotten both the name and author of my best example: the story of a man who is enabled to travel into the future, because himself, in that future when he shall have discovered a method of time-travel, comes back to himself in the present (then, of course, the past) and fetches him.* Less comic, but a more strenuous game, is the very fine working out of the logical consequences of time-travel in Charles Williams's *Many Dimensions*: where, however, this element is combined with many others.

Secondly, the impossible may be simply a postulate to liberate farcical consequences, as in F. Anstey's *Brass Bottle*. The Garuda Stone in his *Vice Versa* is not so pure an example; a serious moral and, indeed, something not far from pathos come in— perhaps against the author's wish.

Sometimes it is a postulate which liberates consequences very far from comic, and, when this is so, if the story is good it will usually point a moral: of itself, without any didactic manipulation by the author on the conscious level. Stevenson's *Dr Jekyll and Mr Hyde* would be an example. Another is Marc Brandel's *Cast the First Shadow*, where a man, long solitary, despised, and oppressed, because he had no shadow, at last meets a woman who shares his innocent defect, but later turns from her in disgust and indignation on finding that she has, in addition, the loathsome and unnatural property of having no reflection. Readers who do not write themselves often describe such stories as allegories, but I doubt if it is as allegories that they arise in the author's mind.

In all these the impossibility is, as I have said, a postulate, something to be granted before the story gets going. Within that frame we inhabit the known world and are as realistic as anyone else. But in the next type (and the last I shall deal with) the marvellous is in the grain of the whole work. We are, throughout, in another world. What makes that world valuable is not, of

---

*Lewis is thinking, I believe, of Robert A. Heinlein's 'By His Boot-straps' in *Spectrum: A Science Fiction Anthology* (1961).

course, mere multiplication of the marvellous either for comic effect (as in *Baron Munchausen* and sometimes in Ariosto and Boiardo) or for mere astonishment (as, I think, in the worst of the *Arabian Nights* or in some children's stories), but its quality, its flavour. If good novels are comments on life, good stories of this sort (which are very much rarer) are actual additions to life; they give, like certain rare dreams, sensations we never had before, and enlarge our conception of the range of possible experience. Hence the difficulty of discussing them at all with those who refuse to be taken out of what they call 'real life'—which means, perhaps, the groove through some far wider area of possible experience to which our senses and our biological, social, or economic interests usually confine us—or, if taken, can see nothing outside it but aching boredom or sickening monstrosity. They shudder and ask to go home. Specimens of this kind, at its best, will never be common. I would include parts of the *Odyssey*, the *Hymn to Aphrodite*, much of the *Kalevala* and *The Faerie Queene*, some of Malory (but none of Malory's best work) and more of *Huon*, parts of Novalis's *Heinrich von Ofterdingen*, *The Ancient Mariner* and *Christabel*, Beckford's *Vathek*, Morris's *Jason* and the *Prologue* (little else) of the *Earthly Paradise*, MacDonald's *Phantastes, Lilith*, and *The Golden Key*, Eddison's *Worm Ouroboros*, Tolkien's *Lord of the Rings*, and that shattering, intolerable, and irresistible work, David Lindsay's *Voyage to Arcturus*. Also Mervyn Peake's *Titus Groan*. Some of Ray Bradbury's stories perhaps make the grade. W. H. Hodgson's *The Night Land* would have made it in eminence from the unforgettable sombre splendour of the images it presents, if it were not disfigured by a sentimental and irrelevant erotic interest and by a foolish, and flat archaism of style. (I do not mean that all archaism is foolish, and have never seen the modern hatred of it cogently defended. If archaism succeeds in giving us the sense of having entered a remote world, it justifies itself. Whether it is correct by philological standards does not then matter a rap.)

I am not sure that anyone has satisfactorily explained the keen, lasting, and solemn pleasure which such stories can give. Jung, who went furthest, seems to me to produce as his explanation one more myth which affects us in the same way as

On Science Fiction

the rest. Surely the analysis of water should not itself be wet? I shall not attempt to do what Jung failed to do. But I would like to draw attention to a neglected fact: the astonishing intensity of the dislike which some readers feel for the mythopoeic. I first found it out by accident. A lady (and, what makes the story more piquant, she herself was a Jungian psychologist by profession) had been talking about a dreariness which seemed to be creeping over her life, the drying up in her of the power to feel pleasure, the aridity of her mental landscape. Drawing a bow at a venture, I asked, 'Have you any taste for fantasies and fairy tales?' I shall never forget how her muscles tightened, her hands clenched themselves, her eyes started as if with horror, and her voice changed, as she hissed out, 'I *loathe* them'. Clearly we here have to do not with a critical opinion but with something like a phobia. And I have seen traces of it elsewhere, though never quite so violent. On the other side, I know from my own experience, that those who like the mythopoeic like it with almost equal intensity. The two phenomena, taken together, should at least dispose of the theory that it is something trivial. It would seem from the reactions it produces, that the mythopoeic is rather, for good or ill, a mode of imagination which does something to us at a deep level. If some seem to go to it in almost compulsive need, others seem to be in terror of what they may meet there. But that is of course only suspicion. What I feel far more sure of is the critical *caveat* which I propounded a while ago. Do not criticise what you have no taste for without great caution. And, above all, do not ever criticise what you simply can't stand. I will lay all the cards on the table. I have long since discovered my own private *phobia*: the thing I can't bear in literature, the thing which makes me profoundly uncomfortable, is the representation of anything like a quasi love affair between two children. It embarrasses and nauseates me. But of course I regard this not as a charter to write slashing reviews of books in which the hated theme occurs, but as a warning not to pass judgement on them at all. For my reaction is unreasonable: such child-loves quite certainly occur in real life and I can give no reason why they should not be represented in art. If they touch the scar of some early *trauma* in me, that is my misfortune. And I would venture to advise all who are attempting

67

to become critics to adopt the same principle. A violent and actually resentful reaction to all books of a certain kind, or to situations of a certain kind, is a danger signal. For I am convinced that good adverse criticism is the most difficult thing we have to do. I would advise everyone to begin it under the most favourable conditions: this is, where you thoroughly know and heartily like the thing the author is trying to do, and have enjoyed many books where it was done well. Then you will have some chance of really showing that he has failed and perhaps even of showing why. But if our real reaction to a book is 'Ugh! I just can't bear this sort of thing,' then I think we shall not be able to diagnose whatever real faults it has. We may labour to conceal our emotion, but we shall end in a welter of emotive, unanalysed, vogue-words— 'arch', 'facetious', 'bogus', 'adolescent', 'immature', and the rest. When we really know what is wrong we need none of these.

A Reply to
Professor Haldane

Before attempting a reply to Professor Haldane's 'Auld Hornie,
F.R.S.', in *The Modern Quarterly*, I had better note the one point of
agreement between us. I think, from the Professor's complaint
that my characters are 'like slugs in an experimental cage who get
a cabbage if they turn right and an electric shock if they turn left',
he suspects me of finding the sanctions of conduct in reward and
punishment. His suspicion is erroneous. I share his detestation for
any such view and his preference for Stoic or Confucian ethics.
Although I believe in an omnipotent God I do not consider that
His omnipotence could in itself create the least obligation to obey
Him. In my romances the 'good' characters are in fact rewarded.
That is because I consider a happy ending appropriate to the
light, holiday kind of fiction I was attempting. The Professor has
mistaken the 'poetic justice' of romance for an ethical theorem. I
would go further. Detestation for any ethic which worships
success is one of my chief reasons for disagreeing with most
communists. In my experience they tend, when all else fails, to
tell me that I ought to forward the revolution because 'it is bound
to come'. One dissuaded me from my own position on the
shockingly irrelevant ground that if I continued to hold it I
should, in good time, be 'mown down'—argued, as a cancer
might argue if it could talk, that he must be right because he
could kill me. I gladly recognise the difference between Professor
Haldane and such communists as that. I ask him, in return, to

recognise the difference between my Christian ethics and those, say, of Paley. There are, on his side as well as on mine, Vichy-like vermin who define the right side as the side that is going to win. Let us put them out of the room before we begin talking.

My chief criticism of the Professor's article is that, wishing to criticise my philosophy (if I may give it so big a name) he almost ignores the books in which I have attempted to set it out and concentrates on my romances. He was told in the preface to *That Hideous Strength* that the doctrines behind that romance could be found, stripped of their fictional masquerade, in *The Abolition of Man*. Why did he not go there to find them? The result of his method is unfortunate. As a philosophical critic the Professor would have been formidable and therefore useful. As a literary critic—though even there he cannot be dull—he keeps on missing the point. A good deal of my reply must therefore be concerned with removal of mere misunderstandings.

His attack resolves itself into three main charges. (1) That my science is usually wrong; (2) that I traduce scientists; (3) that on my view scientific planning 'can only lead to Hell' (and that therefore I am 'a most useful prop to the existing social order', dear to those who 'stand to lose by social changes' and reluctant, for bad motives, to speak out about usury).

(1) My science is usually wrong. Why, yes. So is the Professor's history. He tells us in *Possible Worlds* (1927) that 'five hundred years ago ... it was not clear that celestial distances were so much greater than terrestrial'. But the astronomical text-book which the Middle Ages used, Ptolemy's *Almagest*, had clearly stated (I.v.) that in relation to the distance of the fixed stars the whole Earth must be treated as a mathematical point and had explained on what observations this conclusion was based. The doctrine was well known to King Alfred and even to the author of a 'popular' book like the *South English Legendary*. Again, in 'Auld Hornie', the Professor seems to think that Dante was exceptional in his views on gravitation and the rotundity of the Earth. But the most popular and orthodox authority whom Dante could have consulted, and who died a year or so before his birth, was Vincent of Beauvais. And in his *Speculum Naturale* (VII. vii.) we learn that if there were a hole right through the terrestrial globe (*terre globus*)

and you dropped a stone into that hole, it would come to rest at the centre. In other words, the Professor is about as good a historian as I am a scientist. The difference is that his false history is produced in works intended to be true, whereas my false science is produced in romances. I wanted to write about imaginary worlds. Now that the whole of our own planet has been explored other planets are the only place where you can put them. I needed for my purpose just enough popular astronomy to create in 'the common reader' a 'willing suspension of disbelief'. No one hopes, in such fantasies, to satisfy a real scientist, any more than the writer of a historical romance hopes to satisfy a real archaeologist. (Where the latter effort is seriously made, as in *Romola*, it usually spoils the book.) There is thus a great deal of scientific falsehood in my stories: some of it known to be false even by me when I wrote the books. The canals in Mars are there not because I believe in them but because they are part of the popular tradition; the astrological character of the planets for the same reason. The poet, Sidney says, is the only writer who never lies, because he alone never claims truth for his statements. Or, if 'poet' be too high a term to use in such a context, we can put it another way. The Professor has caught me carving a toy elephant and criticises it as if my aim had been to teach zoology. But what I was after was not the elephant as known to science but our old friend Jumbo.

(2) I think Professor Haldane himself probably regarded his critique of my science as mere skirmishing; with his second charge (that I traduce scientists) we reach something more serious. And here, most unhappily, he concentrates on the wrong book—*That Hideous Strength*—missing the strong point of his own case. If any of my romances could be plausibly accused of being a libel on scientists it would be *Out of the Silent Planet*. It certainly is an attack, if not on scientists, yet on something which might be called 'scientism'—a certain outlook on the world which is casually connected with the popularisation of the sciences, though it is much less common among real scientists than among their readers. It is, in a word, the belief that the supreme moral end is the perpetuation of our own species, and that this is to be pursued even if, in the process of being fitted for survival, our species has to be stripped of all those things for

which we value it—of pity, of happiness, and of freedom. I am not sure that you will find this belief formally asserted by any writer: such things creep in as assumed, and unstated, major premises. But I thought I could feel its approach; in Shaw's *Back to Methuselah*, in Stapledon, and in Professor Haldane's 'Last Judgement' (in *Possible Worlds*). I had noted, of course, that the Professor dissociates his own ideal from that of his Venerites. He says that his own ideal is 'somewhere in between' them and a race 'absorbed in the pursuit of individual happiness'. The 'pursuit of individual happiness' is, I trust, intended to mean 'the pursuit by each individual of his own happiness at the expense of his neighbour's'. But it might also be taken to support the (to me meaningless) view that there is some other kind of happiness— that something other than an individual is capable of happiness or misery. I also suspected (was I wrong?) that the Professor's 'somewhere in between' came pretty near the Venerite end of the scale. It was against this outlook on life, this ethic, if you will, that I wrote my satiric fantasy, projecting in my Weston a buffoon-villain image of the 'metabiological' heresy. If anyone says that to make him a scientist was unfair, since the view I am attacking is not chiefly rampant among scientists, I might agree with him: though I think such a criticism would be over-sensitive. The odd thing is that Professor Haldane thinks Weston 'recognisable as a scientist'. I am relieved, for I had doubts about him. If I were briefed to attack my own books I should have pointed out that though Weston, for the sake of the plot, has to be a physicist, his interests seem to be exclusively biological. I should also have asked whether it was credible that such a gas-bag could ever have invented a mouse-trap, let alone a space-ship. But then, I wanted farce as well as fantasy.

Perelandra, in so far as it does not merely continue its predecessor, is mainly for my co-religionists. Its real theme would not interest Professor Haldane, I think, one way or the other. I will only point out that if he had noticed the very elaborate ritual in which the angels hand over the rule of that planet to the humans he might have realised that the 'angelocracy' pictured on Mars is, for me, a thing of the past: the Incarnation has made a difference. I do not mean that he can be expected to be interested in this view as such: but it might have saved us from at least one political red herring.

That Hideous Strength he has almost completely misunderstood. The 'good' scientist is put in precisely to show that 'scientists' as such are not the target. To make the point clearer, he leaves my N.I.C.E. because he finds he was wrong in his original belief that 'it had something to do with science' (p.83). To make it clearer yet, my principal character, the man almost irresistibly attracted by the N.I.C.E. is described (p. 226) as one whose 'education had been neither scientific nor classical—merely "Modern". The severities both of abstraction and of high human tradition had passed him by.... He was ... a glib examinee in subjects that require no exact knowledge.' To make it doubly and trebly clear the rake's progress of Wither's mind is represented (p. 438) as philosophical, not scientific at all. Lest even this should not be enough, the hero (who is, by the way, to some extent a fancy portrait of a man I know, but not of me) is made to say that the sciences are 'good and innocent in themselves' (p. 248), though evil 'scientism' is creeping into them. And finally, what we are obviously up against throughout the story is not scientists but *officials*. If anyone ought to feel himself libelled by this book it is not the scientist but the civil servant: and, next to the civil servant, certain philosophers. Frost is the mouthpiece of Professor Waddington's ethical theories: by which I do not, of course, mean that Professor Waddington in real life is a man like Frost.

What, then, was I attacking? Firstly, a certain view about values: the attack will be found, undisguised, in *The Abolition of Man*. Secondly, I was saying, like St James and Professor Haldane, that to be a friend of 'the World' is to be an enemy of God. The difference between us is that the Professor sees the 'World' purely in terms of those threats and those allurements which depend on money. I do not. The most 'worldly' society I have ever lived in is that of schoolboys: most worldly in the cruelty and arrogance of the strong, the toadyism and mutual treachery of the weak, and the unqualified snobbery of both. Nothing was so base that most members of the school proletariat would not do it, or suffer it, to win the favour of the school aristocracy: hardly any injustice too bad for the aristocracy to practise. But the class system did not in the least depend on the amount of pocket money. Who needs to care about money if most of the things he wants will be offered by cringing servility and the remainder can be taken by force? This lesson has remained with me all my life. That is one of the reasons why I cannot share Professor Haldane's exaltation at the banishment of Mammon from 'a sixth of our planet's surface'. I have already lived in a world from which Mammon was banished: it was the most wicked and miserable I have yet known. If Mammon were the only devil, it would be another matter. But where Mammon vacates the throne, how if Moloch takes his place? As Aristotle said, 'Men do not become tyrants in order to keep warm'. All men, of course, desire pleasure and safety. But all men also desire power and all men desire the mere sense of being 'in the know' or the 'inner ring', of not being 'outsiders': a passion insufficiently studied and the chief theme of my story. When the state of society is such that money is the passport to all these prizes, then of course money will be the prime temptation. But when the passport changes, the desires will remain. And there are many other possible passports: position in an official hierarchy, for instance. Even now, the ambitious and worldly man would not inevitably choose the post with the higher salary. The pleasure of being 'high up and far within' may be worth the sacrifice of some income.

(3) Thirdly, was I attacking scientific planning? According to Professor Haldane 'Mr. Lewis's idea is clear enough. The application of science to human affairs can only lead to Hell'. There is certainly no warrant for 'can only'; but he is justified in assuming that unless I had thought I saw a serious and widespread danger I would not have given planning so central a place even in what I called a 'fairy tale' and a 'tall story'. But if you must reduce the romance to a proposition, the proposition would be almost the converse of that which the Professor supposes: not 'scientific planning will certainly lead to Hell', but 'Under modern conditions any effective invitation to Hell will certainly appear in the guise of scientific planning'—as Hitler's regime in fact did. Every tyrant must begin by claiming to have what his victims respect and to give what they want. The

majority in most modern countries respect science and want to be planned. And, therefore, almost by definition, if any man or group wishes to enslave us it will of course describe itself as 'scientific planned democracy'. It may be true that any real salvation must equally, though by hypothesis truthfully, describe itself as 'scientific planned democracy'. All the more reason to look very carefully at anything which bears that label.

My fears of such a tyranny will seem to the Professor either insincere or pusillanimous. For him the danger is all in the opposite direction, in the chaotic selfishness of individualism. I must try to explain why I fear more the disciplined cruelty of some ideological oligarchy. The Professor has his own explanation of this; he thinks I am unconsciously motivated by the fact that I 'stand to lose by social change'. And indeed it would be hard for me to welcome a change which might well consign me to a concentration camp. I might add that it would be likewise easy for the Professor to welcome a change which might place him in the highest rank of an omnicompetent oligarchy. That is why the motive game is so uninteresting. Each side can go on playing *ad nauseam*, but when all the mud has been flung every man's views still remain to be considered on their merits. I decline the motive game and resume the discussion. I do not hope to make Professor Haldane agree with me. But I should like him at least to understand why I think devil worship a real possibility.

I am a democrat. Professor Haldane thinks I am not, but he bases his opinion on a passage in *Out of the Silent Planet* where I am discussing, not the relations of a species to itself (politics) but the relations of one species to another. His interpretation, if consistently worked out, would attribute to me the doctrine that horses are fit for an equine monarchy though not for an equine democracy. Here, as so often, what I was really saying was something which the Professor, had he understood it, would have found simply uninteresting.

I am a democrat because I believe that no man or group of men is good enough to be trusted with uncontrolled power over others. And the higher the pretensions of such power, the more dangerous I think it both to the rulers and to the subjects. Hence Theocracy is the worst of all governments. If we must have a tyrant a robber baron is far better than an inquisitor. The baron's cruelty may sometimes sleep, his cupidity at some point be sated; and since he dimly knows he is doing wrong he may possibly repent. But the inquisitor who mistakes his own cruelty and lust of power and fear for the voice of Heaven will torment us infinitely because he torments us with the approval of his own conscience and his better impulses appear to him as temptations. And since Theocracy is the worst, the nearer any government approaches to Theocracy the worse it will be. A metaphysic, held by the rulers with the force of a religion, is a bad sign. It forbids them, like the inquisitor, to admit any grain of truth or good in their opponents, it abrogates the ordinary rules of morality, and it gives a seemingly high, super-personal sanction to all the very ordinary human passions by which, like other men, the rulers will frequently be actuated. In a word, it forbids wholesome doubt. A political programme can never in reality be more than probably right. We never know all the facts about the present and we can only guess the future. To attach to a party programme—whose highest real claim is to reasonable prudence—the sort of assent which we should reserve for demonstrable theorems, is a kind of intoxication.

This false certainty comes out in Professor Haldane's article. He simply cannot believe that a man could really be in doubt about usury. I have no objection to his thinking me wrong. What shocks me is his instantaneous assumption that the question is so simple that there could be no real hesitation about it. It is breaking Aristotle's canon—to demand in every enquiry that degree of certainty which the subject matter allows. And not *on your life* to pretend that you see further than you do.

Being a democrat, I am opposed to all very drastic and sudden changes of society (in whatever direction) because they never in fact take place except by a particular technique. That technique involves the seizure of power by a small, highly disciplined group of people; the terror and the secret police follow, it would seem, automatically. I do not think any group good enough to have such power. They are men of like passions with ourselves. The secrecy and discipline of their organisation will have already inflamed in them that passion for the inner ring which I think at least as corrupting as avarice; and their high ideological pretensions will have lent all their passions the dangerous prestige of the Cause. Hence, in whatever direction the change is made, it is for me damned by its *modus operandi*. The worst of all public dangers is the committee of public safety. The character in *That Hideous Strength* whom the Professor never mentions is Miss Hardcastle, the chief of the secret police. She is the common factor in all revolutions; and, as she says, you won't get anyone to do her job well unless they get some kick out of it.

I must, of course, admit that the actual state of affairs may sometimes be so bad that a man is tempted to risk change even by revolutionary methods; to say that desperate diseases require desperate remedies and that necessity knows no law. But to yield to this temptation is, I think, fatal. It is under that pretext that every abomination enters. Hitler, the Machiavellian Prince, the Inquisition, the Witch Doctor, all claimed to be necessary.

From this point of view is it impossible that the Professor could come to understand what I mean by devil worship, as a symbol? For me it is not merely a symbol. Its relation to the reality is more complicated, and it would not interest Professor Haldane. But it is at least partly symbolical and I will try to give the Professor such an account of my meaning as can be grasped without introducing the supernatural. I have to begin by correcting a rather curious misunderstanding. When we accuse people of devil worship we do not usually mean that they knowingly worship the devil. That, I agree, is a rare perversion. When a rationalist accuses certain Christians, say, the seventeenth-century Calvinists, of devil worship, he does not mean that they worshipped a being whom they regarded as the devil; he means that they worshipped as God a being whose character the rationalist thinks diabolical. It is clearly in that sense, and that sense only, that my Frost worships devils. He adores the 'macrobes' because they are beings stronger, and therefore to him 'higher', than men: worships them, in fact, on the same grounds on which my communist friend would have me favour the revolution. No man at present is (probably) doing what I represent Frost as doing: but he is the ideal point at which certain lines of tendency already observable will meet if produced.

The first of these tendencies is the growing exaltation of the collective and the growing indifference to persons. The philosophical sources are probably in Rousseau and Hegel, but the general character of modern life with its huge impersonal organisations may be more potent than any philosophy. Professor Haldane himself illustrates the present state of mind very well. He thinks that if one were inventing a language for 'sinless beings who loved their neighbours as themselves' it would be appropriate to have no words for 'my', 'I', and 'other personal pronouns and inflexions'. In other words he sees no difference between two opposite solutions of the problem of selfishness: between love (which is a relation between persons) and the abolition of persons. Nothing but a *Thou* can be loved and a *Thou* can exist only for an *I*. A society in which no one was conscious of himself as a person over against other persons, where none could say 'I love you', would, indeed, be free from selfishness, but not through love. It would be 'unselfish' as a bucket of water is unselfish. Another good example comes in *Back to Methuselah*. There, as soon as Eve has learned that generation is possible, she says to Adam, 'You may die as soon as I have made a new Adam. Not before. But then as soon as you like.' The individual does not matter. And therefore when we really get going (shreds of an earlier ethic still cling to most minds) it will not matter what you do to an individual.

Secondly, we have the emergence of 'the Party' in the modern sense—the Fascists, Nazis, or Communists. What distinguishes this from the political parties of the nineteenth century is the belief of its members that they are not merely trying to carry out a programme, but are obeying an impersonal force: that Nature, or Evolution, or the Dialectic, or the Race, is carrying them on. This tends to be accompanied by two beliefs which cannot, so far as I see, be reconciled in logic but which blend very easily on the emotional level: the belief that the process which the Party embodies is inevitable, and the belief that the forwarding of this process is the supreme duty and abrogates all ordinary moral laws. In this state of mind men can become devil-worshippers in the sense that they can now *honour*, as well as obey, their own vices. All men at times obey their vices: but it is when cruelty, envy, and lust of power appear as the commands of a great super-personal force that they can be exercised with self-approval. The first symptom is in language. When to 'kill' becomes to 'liquidate' the process has begun. The pseudo-scientific word disinfects the thing of blood and tears, or pity and shame, and mercy itself can be regarded as a sort of untidiness.

[Lewis goes on to say: 'It is, at present, in their sense of serving a metaphysical force that the modern 'Parties' approximate most closely to religions. Odinism in Germany, or the cult of Lenin's corpse in Russia are probably less important but there is quite a . . . '—and here the manuscript ends. One page (I think no more) is missing. It was probably lost soon after the essay was written, and without Lewis's knowledge, for he had, characteristically, folded the manuscript and scribbled the title 'Anti-Haldane' on one side with a pencil.]

The Hobbit

The publishers claim that *The Hobbit*, though very unlike *Alice*, resembles it in being the work of a professor at play. A more important truth is that both belong to a very small class of books which have nothing in common save that each admits us to a world of its own—a world that seems to have been going on before we stumbled into it but which, once found by the right reader, becomes indispensable to him. Its place is with *Alice*, *Flatland*, *Phantastes*, *The Wind in the Willows*.

To define the world of *The Hobbit* is, of course, impossible, because it is new. You cannot anticipate it before you go there, as you cannot forget it once you have gone. The author's admirable illustrations and maps of Mirkwood and Goblingate and Esgaroth give one an inkling—and so do the names of the dwarf and dragon that catch our eyes as we first ruffle the pages. But there are dwarfs and dwarfs, and no common recipe for children's stories will give you creatures so rooted in their own soil and history as those of Professor Tolkien—who obviously knows much more about them than he needs for this tale. Still less will the common recipe prepare us for the curious shift from the matter-of-fact beginnings of his story ('hobbits are small people, smaller than dwarfs—and they have no beards—but very much larger than Lilliputians')* to the saga-like tone of the later chapters ('It is in my mind to ask what share of their inheritance you would have paid had you found the hoard ungarded').† You must read for

---

The Hobbit: or There and Back Again (1937), ch. I.
†*Ibid.*, ch. XV.

yourself to find out how inevitable the change is and how it keeps pace with the hero's journey. Though all is marvellous, nothing is arbitrary: all the inhabitants of Wilderland seem to have the same unquestionable right to their existence as those of our own world, though the fortunate child who meets them will have no notion—and his unlearned elders not much more—of the deep sources in our blood and tradition from which they spring.

For it must be understood that this is a children's book only in the sense that the first of many readings can be undertaken in the nursery. *Alice* is read gravely by children and with laughter by grown-ups; *The Hobbit*, on the other hand, will be funniest to its youngest readers, and only years later, at a tenth or a twentieth reading, will they begin to realise what deft scholarship and profound reflection have gone to make everything in it so ripe, so friendly, and in its own way so true. Prediction is dangerous: but *The Hobbit* may well prove a classic.

Tolkien's
The Lord of the Rings

This book[*] is like lightning from a clear sky; as sharply different, as unpredictable in our age as *Songs of Innocence* were in theirs. To say that in it heroic romance, gorgeous, eloquent, and unashamed, has suddenly returned at a period almost pathological in its anti-romanticism is inadequate. To us, who live in that odd period, the return—and the sheer relief of it—is doubtless the important thing. But in the history of Romance itself—a history which stretches back to the *Odyssey* and beyond—it makes not a return but an advance or revolution: the conquest of new territory.

Nothing quite like it was ever done before. 'One takes it', says Naomi Mitchison, 'as seriously as Malory'.[†] But then the ineluctable sense of reality which we feel in the *Morte d'Arthur* comes largely from the great weight of other men's work built up century by century, which has gone into it. The utterly new achievement of Professor Tolkien is that he carries a comparable sense of reality unaided. Probably no book yet written in the world is quite such a radical instance of what its author has

---

[*]*The Fellowship of the Ring* (1954), the first volume of the trilogy *The Lord of the Rings*. The other volumes, *The Two Towers* and *The Return of the King* were published in 1955. Tolkien was later to revise the whole work for a hardback second edition (1966).

[†] 'One Ring to Bind Them', *New Statesman and Nation* (18 September 1954).

elsewhere called 'sub-creation'.* The direct debt (there are of course subtler kinds of debt) which every author must owe to the actual universe is here deliberately reduced to the minimum. Not content to create his own story, he creates, with an almost insolent prodigality, the whole world in which it is to move, with its own theology, myths, geography, history, palaeography, languages, and orders of beings—a world 'full of strange creatures beyond count'.† The names alone are a feast, whether redolent of quiet countryside (Michel Delving, South Farthing), tall and kingly (Boramir, Faramir, Elendil), loathsome like Smeagol, who is also Gollum, or frowning in the evil strength of Barad Dur or Gorgoroth; yet best of all (Lothlorien, Gilthoniel, Galadriel) when they embody that piercing, high elvish beauty of which no other prose writer has captured so much.

Such a book has of course its predestined readers, even now more numerous and more critical than is always realised. To them a reviewer need say little, except that here are beauties which pierce like swords or burn like cold iron; here is a book that will break your heart. They will know that this is good news, good beyond hope. To complete their happiness one need only add that it promises to be gloriously long: this volume is only the first of three. But it is too great a book to rule only its natural subjects. Something must be said to 'those without', to the unconverted. At the very least, possible misunderstandings may be got out of the way.

First, we must clearly understand that though *The Fellowship* in one way continues its author's fairy tale, *The Hobbit*, it is in no sense an overgrown 'juvenile'. The truth is the other way round. *The Hobbit* was merely a fragment torn from the author's huge myth and adapted for children; inevitably losing something by the adaptation. *The Fellowship* gives us at last the lineaments of that myth 'in their true dimensions like themselves'. Misunderstanding on this point might easily be encouraged by the first chapter, in which the author (taking a risk) writes almost in the manner of the earlier and far lighter book. With some who will

---

* 'On Fairy-Stories' in *Essays Presented to Charles Williams* (1947).
† 'Prologue', *The Fellowship of the Ring*.

find the main body of the book deeply moving, this chapter may not be a favourite.

Yet there were good reasons for such an opening; still more for the Prologue (wholly admirable, this) which precedes it. It is essential that we should first be well steeped in the 'homeliness', the frivolity, even (in its best sense) the vulgarity of the creatures called Hobbits; these unambitious folk, peaceable yet almost anarchical, with faces 'good-natured rather than beautiful' and 'mouths apt to laughter and eating',* who treat smoking as an art and like books which tell them what they already know. They are not an allegory of the English, but they are perhaps a myth that only an Englishman (or, should we add, a Dutchman?) could have created. Almost the central theme of the book is the contrast between the Hobbits (or 'the Shire') and the appalling destiny to which some of them are called, the terrifying discovery that the humdrum happiness of the Shire, which they had taken for granted as something normal, is in reality a sort of local and temporary accident, that its existence depends on being protected by powers which Hobbits dare not imagine, that any Hobbit may find himself forced out of the Shire and caught up into that high conflict. More strangely still, the event of that conflict between strongest things may come to depend on him, who is almost the weakest.

What shows that we are reading myth, not allegory, is that there are no pointers to a specifically theological, or political, or psychological application. A myth points, for each reader, to the realm he lives in most. It is a master key; use it on what door you like. And there are other themes in *The Fellowship* equally serious.

That is why no catchwords about 'escapism' or 'nostalgia' and no distrust of 'private worlds' are in court. This is no Angria, no dreaming; it is sane and vigilant invention, revealing at point after point the integration of the author's mind. What is the use of calling 'private' a world we can all walk into and test and in which we find such a balance? As for escapism, what we chiefly escape is the illusions of our ordinary life. We certainly do not escape

---

* *Ibid.*

anguish. Despite many a snug fireside and many an hour of good cheer to gratify the Hobbit in each of us, anguish is, for me, almost the prevailing note. But not, as in the literature most typical of our age, the anguish of abnormal or contorted souls: rather that anguish of those who were happy before a certain darkness came up and will be happy if they live to see it gone.

Nostalgia does indeed come in; not ours nor the author's, but that of the characters. It is closely connected with one of Professor Tolkien's greatest achievements. One would have supposed that diuturnity was the quality least likely to be found in an invented world. And one has, in fact, an uneasy feeling that the worlds of the *Furioso* or *The Water of the Wondrous Isles* weren't there at all before the curtain rose. But in the Tolkienian world you can hardly put your foot down anywhere from Esgaroth to Forlindon or between Ered Mithrin and Khand, without stirring the dust of history. Our own world, except at certain rare moments, hardly seems so heavy with its past. This is one element in the anguish which the characters bear. But with the anguish there comes also a strange exaltation. They are at once stricken and upheld by the memory of vanished civilisations and lost splendour. They have outlived the second and third Ages; the wine of life was drawn long since. As we read we find ourselves sharing their burden; when we have finished, we return to our own life not relaxed but fortified.

But there is more in the book still. Every now and then, risen from sources we can only conjecture and almost alien (one would think) to the author's habitual imagination, figures meet us so brimming with life (not human life) that they make our sort of anguish and our sort of exaltation seem unimportant. Such is Tom Bombadil, such the unforgettable Ents. This is surely the utmost reach of invention, when an author produces what seems to be not even his own, much less anyone else's. Is mythopoeia, after all, not the most, but the least, subjective of activities?

Even now I have left out almost everything—the silvan leafiness, the passions, the high virtues, the remote horizons. Even if I had space I could hardly convey them. And after all the most obvious appeal of the book is perhaps also its deepest: 'there was sorrow then too, and gathering dark, but great valour, and

great deeds that were not wholly vain'.* *Not wholly vain*—it is the
cool middle point between illusion and disillusionment.

When I reviewed the first volume of this work I hardly dared
to hope it would have the success which I was sure it deserved.
Happily I am proved wrong. There is, however, one piece of false
criticism which had better be answered; the complaint that the
characters are all either black or white. Since the climax of
Volume I was mainly concerned with the struggle between good
and evil in the mind of Boromir, it is not easy to see how anyone
could have said this. I will hazard a guess. 'How shall a man
judge what to do in such times?' asks someone in Volume II. 'As
he has ever judged', comes the reply. 'Good and ill have not
changed . . . nor are they one thing among Elves and Dwarves and
another among Men.'†

This is the basis of the whole Tolkienian world. I think some
readers, seeing (and disliking) this rigid demarcation of black and
white, imagine they have seen a rigid demarcation between black
and white people. Looking at the squares, they assume (in
defiance of the facts) that all the pieces must be making bishops'
moves which confine them to one colour. But even such readers
will hardly brazen it out through the two last volumes. Motives,
even in the right side, are mixed. Those who are now traitors
usually began with comparatively innocent intentions. Heroic
Rohan and imperial Gondor are partly diseased. Even the
wretched Smeagol, till quite late in the story, has good impulses;
and (by a tragic paradox) what finally pushes him over the brink
is an unpremeditated speech by the most selfless character of all.

There are two Books in each volume and now that all six are
before us the very high architectural quality of the romance is
revealed. Book I builds up the main theme. In Book II that
theme, enriched with much retrospective material, continues.
Then comes the change. In III and V the fate of the company, now
divided, becomes entangled with a huge complex of forces which
are grouping and re-grouping themselves in relation to Mordor.

---

* *Ibid.*, Bk. I, ch. 2.
† *The Two Towers*, Bk. III, ch. 2.

The main theme, isolated from this, occupies IV and the early part of VI (the latter part of course giving all the resolutions). But we are never allowed to forget the intimate connection between it and the rest. On the one hand, the whole world is going to the war; the story rings with galloping hoofs, trumpets, steel on steel. On the other, very far away, miserable figures creep (like mice on a slag heap) through the twilight of Mordor. And all the time we know the fate of the world depends far more on the small movement than on the great. This is a structural invention of the highest order: it adds immensely to the pathos, irony, and grandeur of the tale.

Yet those Books are not in the least inferior. Of picking out great moments (such as the cock-crow at the Siege of Gondor) there would be no end; I will mention two general (and totally different) excellences. One, surprisingly, is realisms. This war has the very quality of the war my generation knew. It is all here: the endless, unintelligible movement, the sinister quiet of the front when 'everything is now ready', the flying civilians, the lively, vivid friendships, the background of something like despair and the merry foreground, and such heaven-sent windfalls as a *cache* of choice tobacco 'salvaged' from a ruin. The author has told us elsewhere that his taste for fairy tale was wakened into maturity by active service;* that, no doubt, is why we can say of his war scenes (quoting Gimli the Dwarf), 'There is good rock here. This country has tough bones'.† The other excellence is that no individual, and no species, seems to exist only for the sake of the plot. All exist in their own right and would have been worth creating for their mere flavour even if they had been irrelevant. Treebeard would have served any other author (if any other could have conceived him) for a whole book. His eyes are 'filled up with ages of memory and long, slow, steady thinking'.‡ Through those ages his name has grown with him, so that he cannot now tell it; it would, by now, take too long to pronounce. When he learns that the thing they are standing on is a hill, he complains that

---

* 'On Fairy-Stories'.
† *The Two Towers*, Bk. III, ch. 2.
‡ *Ibid.*, Bk. III, ch. 4.

this is but 'a hasty word'* for that which has so much history in it.

How far Treebeard can be regarded as a 'portrait of the artist' must remain doubtful; but when he hears that some people want to identify the Ring with the hydrogen bomb, and Mordor with Russia, I think he might call it a 'hasty' word. How long do people think a world like his takes to grow? Do they think it can be done as quickly as a modern nation changes its Public Enemy Number One or as modern scientists invent new weapons? When Professor Tolkien began there was probably no nuclear fission and the contemporary incarnation of Mordor was a good deal nearer our shores. But the text itself teaches us that Sauron is eternal; the war of the Ring is only one of a thousand wars against him. Every time we shall be wise to fear his ultimate victory, after which there will be 'no more songs'. Again and again we shall have good evidence that 'the wind is setting East, and the withering of all woods may be drawing near'.† Every time we win we shall know that our victory is impermanent. If we insist on asking for the moral of the story, that is its moral: a recall from facile optimism and wailing pessimism alike, to that hard, yet not quite desperate, insight into Man's unchanging predicament by which heroic ages have lived. It is here that the Norse affinity is strongest; hammer-strokes, but with compassion.

'But why', (some ask), 'why, if you have a serious comment to make on the real life of men, must you do it by talking about a phantasmagoric never-never land of your own?' Because, I take it, one of the main things the author wants to say is that the real life of men is of that mythical and heroic quality. One can see the principle at work in his characterisation. Much that in a realistic work would be done by 'character delineation' is here done simply by making the character an elf, a dwarf, or a hobbit. The imagined beings have their insides on the outside; they are visible souls. And Man as a whole, Man pitted against the universe, have we seen him at all till we see that he is like a hero in a fairy tale? In the book Eomer rashly contrasts 'the green earth' with

---

* *Ibid.*
† *Ibid.*

'legends'. Aragorn replies that the green earth itself is 'a mighty matter of legend'.*

The value of the myth is that it takes all the things we know and restores to them the rich significance which has been hidden by 'the veil of familiarity'. The child enjoys his cold meat (otherwise dull to him) by pretending it is buffalo, just killed with his own bow and arrow. And the child is wise. The real meat comes back to him more savoury for having been dipped in a story; you might say that only then is it the real meat. If you are tired of the real landscape, look at it in a mirror. By putting bread, gold, horse, apple, or the very roads into a myth, we do not retreat from reality: we rediscover it. As long as the story lingers in our mind, the real things are more themselves. This book applies the treatment not only to bread or apple but to good and evil, to our endless perils, our anguish, and our joys. By dipping them in myth we see them more clearly. I do not think he could have done it in any other way.

The book is too original and too opulent for any final judgement on a first reading. But we know at once that it has done things to us. We are not quite the same men. And though we must ration ourselves in our re-readings. I have little doubt that the book will soon take its place among the indispensables.

---

* *Ibid.*, Bk. III, ch. 2.

A Panegyric for Dorothy L. Sayers

The variety of Dorothy Sayers's work makes it almost impossible to find anyone who can deal properly with it all. Charles Williams might have done so; I certainly can't. It is embarrassing to admit that I am no great reader of detective stories: embarrassing because, in our present state of festering intellectual class consciousness, the admission might be taken as a boast. It is nothing of the sort: I respect, though I do not much enjoy, that severe and civilised form, which demands much fundamental brain work of those who write in it and assumes as its background uncorrupted and unbrutalised methods of criminal investigation. Prigs have put it about that Dorothy in later life was ashamed of her 'tekkies' and hated to hear them mentioned. A couple of years ago my wife asked her if this was true and was relieved to hear her deny it. She had stopped working in that genre because she felt she had done all she could with it. And indeed, I gather, a full process of development had taken place. I have heard it said that Lord Peter is the only imaginary detective who ever grew up— grew from the Duke's son, the fabulous amorist, the scholar swashbuckler, and connoisseur of wine, into the increasingly human character, not without quirks and flaws, who loves and marries, and is nursed by, Harriet Vane. Reviewers complained that Miss Sayers was falling in love with her hero. On which a better critic remarked to me, 'It would be truer to say she was

falling out of love with him; and ceased fondling a girl's dream—
if she had ever done so—and began inventing a man.'

There is in reality no cleavage between the detective stories
and her other works. In them, as in it, she is first and foremost
the craftsman, the professional. She always saw herself as one who
has learned a trade, and respects it, and demands respect for it
from others. We who loved her may (among ourselves) lovingly
admit that this attitude was sometimes almost comically empha-
tic. One soon learned that 'We authors, Ma'am',* was the most
acceptable key. Gas about 'inspiration', whimperings about critics
or public, all the paraphernalia of *dandyisme* and 'outsidership'
were, I think, simply disgusting to her. She aspired to be, and
was, at once a popular entertainer and a conscientious craftsman:
like (in her degree) Chaucer, Cervantes, Shakespeare, or Molière. I
have an idea that, with a very few exceptions, it is only such
writers who matter much in the long run. 'One shows one's
greatness', says Pascal, 'not by being at an extremity but by being
simultaneously at two extremities.' Much of her most valuable
thought about writing was embodied in *The Mind of the Maker*: a
book which is still too little read. It has faults. But books about
writing by those who have themselves written viable books are
too rare and too useful to be neglected.

For a Christian, of course, this pride in one's craft, which so
easily withers into pride in oneself, raises a fiercely practical
problem. It is delightfully characteristic of her extremely robust
and forthright nature that she soon lifted this problem to the fully
conscious level and made it the theme of one of her major works.
The architect in *The Zeal of Thy House* is at the outset the
incarnation of—and therefore doubtless the *Catharsis* from—a
possible Dorothy whom the actual Dorothy Sayers was offering for
mortification. His disinterested zeal for the work itself has her
full sympathy. But she knows that, without grace, it is a
dangerous virtue: little better than the 'artistic conscience' which
every Bohemian bungler pleads as a justification for neglecting

---

*This expression, attributed to Benjamin Disraeli, was found to have a
soothing effect upon Queen Victoria who in 1868 published her *Leaves
from a Journal of Our Life in the Highlands*.

his parents, deserting his wife, and cheating his creditors. From the beginning, personal pride is entering into the architect's character: the play records his costly salvation.

As the detective stories do not stand quite apart, so neither do the explicitly religious works. She never sank the artist and entertainer in the evangelist. The very astringent (and admirable) preface to *The Man Born to Be King*, written when she had lately been assailed with a great deal of ignorant and spiteful obloquy, makes the point of view defiantly clear. 'It was assumed', she writes, 'that my object in writing was "to do good". But that was in fact not my object at all, though it was quite properly the object of those who commissioned the plays in the first place. My object was *to tell that story* to the best of my ability, within the medium at my disposal—in short, to make as good a work of art as I could. For a work of art that is not good and true *in art* is not true and good in any other respect.'* Of course, while art and evangelism were distinct, they turned out to demand one another. Bad art on this theme went hand in hand with bad theology. 'Let me tell you, good Christian people, an honest writer would be ashamed to treat a nursery tale as you have treated the greatest drama in history: and this in virtue, not of his faith, but of his calling.'† And equally, of course, her disclaimer of an intention to 'do good' was ironically rewarded by the immense amount of good she evidently did.

The architectonic qualities of this dramatic sequence will hardly be questioned. Some tell me they find it vulgar. Perhaps they do not quite know what they mean; perhaps they have not fully digested the answers to this charge given in the preface. Or perhaps it is simply not 'addressed to their condition'. Different souls take their nourishment in different vessels. For my own part, I have re-read it in every Holy Week since it first appeared, and never re-read it without being deeply moved.

Her later years were devoted to translation. The last letter I ever wrote to her was in acknowledgement of her *Song of Roland*,

---

***The Man Born to Be King: A Play-Cycle on the Life of Our Lord and Saviour Jesus Christ* (1943).
†*Ibid.*

and I was lucky enough to say that the end-stopped lines and utterly unadorned style of the original must have made it a far harder job than Dante. Her delight at this (surely not very profound) remark suggested that she was rather starved for rational criticism. I do not think this one of her most successful works. It is too violently colloquial for my palate; but, then, she knew far more Old French than I. In her Dante* the problem is not quite the same. It should always be read in conjunction with the paper on Dante which she contributed to the *Essays Presented to Charles Williams.*† There you get the first impact of Dante on a mature, a scholarly, and an extremely independent mind. That impact determined the whole character of her translation. She had been startled and delighted by something in Dante for which no critic, and no earlier translator, had prepared her: his sheer narrative impetus, his frequent homeliness, his high comedy, his grotesque buffoonery. These qualities she was determined to preserve at all costs. If, in order to do so, she had to sacrifice sweetness or sublimity, then sacrificed they should be. Hence her audacities in both language and rhythm.

We must distinguish this from something rather discreditable that has been going on of recent years—I mean the attempt of some translators from Greek and Latin to make their readers believe that the *Aeneid* is written in service slang and that Attic Tragedy uses the language of the streets. What such versions implicitly assert is simply false; but what Dorothy was trying to represent by her audacities is quite certainly there in Dante. The question is how far you can do it justice without damage to other qualities which are also there and thus misrepresenting the *Comedy* as much in one direction as fussy, Miltonic old Cary had done in the other.‡ In the end, I suppose, one comes to a choice of

---

*Miss Sayers's translation of Dante's *Divine Comedy* appeared in three volumes: *The Comedy of Dante Alighieri the Florentine. Cantica I: Hell* (1949); *The Comedy of Dante Alighieri the Florentine. Cantica II: Purgatory* (1955); *The Comedy of Dante Alighieri the Florentine. Cantica III: Paradise*, translation with Barbara Reynolds (1962).

†'"...And Telling You a Story": A Note on *The Divine Comedy*', *Essays Presented to Charles Williams* (1947).

‡*The Vision: or Hell, Purgatory and Paradise of Dante Alighieri*, translated by Henry Francis Cary (1910).

evils. No version can give the whole of Dante. So at least I said when I read her *Inferno*. But, then, when I came to the *Purgatorio*, a little miracle seemed to be happening. She had risen, just as Dante himself rose in his second part: growing richer, more liquid, more elevated. Then first I began to have great hopes of her *Paradiso*. Would she go on rising? Was it possible? Dared we hope?

Well. She died instead; went, as one may in all humility hope, to learn more of Heaven than even the *Paradiso* could tell her. For all she did and was, for delight and instruction, for her militant loyalty as a friend, for courage and honesty, for the richly feminine qualities which showed through a port and manner superficially masculine and even gleefully ogreish—let us thank the Author who invented her.

The Mythopoeic Gift of Rider Haggard

I hope Mr Morton Cohen's excellent *Rider Haggard: His Life and Works* will move people to reconsider the whole Haggard question. For there really is a problem here. The vices of his style are inexcusable; the vapidity (and frequency) of his reflections, hard to bear. But it is no longer any good pretending that his best work was merely an ephemeral and commercial success. It has not passed away like the works of Ouida, Mrs Oliphant, Stanley Weyman, or Max Pemberton. It has survived the whole climate of opinion which once made its imperialism and vague pieties acceptable. The promised time 'when the Rudyards cease from Kipling and the Haggards ride no more'* has failed to arrive. Obstinately, scandalously, Haggard continues to be read and re-read. Why?

The significant fact for me is the feeling we have as we close *King Solomon's Mines*, or, still more, *She*. 'If only . . . ' are the words that rise to our lips. If only we could have had this very same story told by a Stevenson, a Tolkien, or a William Golding. If only, *faute de mieux*, we were even allowed to re-write it ourselves!

Note, the very same story. It is not the construction that is faulty. From the move of his first pawn to the final checkmate, Haggard usually plays like a master. His openings—what story in the world opens better than *She*?—are full of alluring promise, and his catastrophes triumphantly keep it.

*J. K. Stephen, 'To R.K.', *Lapsus Calami* (1905).

The lack of detailed character-study is not a fault at all. An adventure story neither needs nor admits it. Even in real life adventures tend to obliterate fine shades. Hardship and danger strip us down to the bare moral essentials. The distinction between shirker and helper, brave and cowardly, trusty and treacherous, overrides everything else. 'Character' in the novelist's sense is a flower that expands fully where people are safe, fed, dry and warmed. That adventure stories remind us of this is one of their merits.

The real defects of Haggard are two. First, he can't write. Or rather (I learn from Mr Cohen) won't. Won't be bothered. Hence the *clichés*, jocosities, frothy eloquence. When he speaks through the mouth of Quatermain he makes some play with the unliterary character of the simple hunter. It never dawned on him that what he wrote in his own person was a great deal worse—'literary' in the most damning sense of the word.

Secondly, the intellectual defects. No one after reading Mr Cohen can believe that Haggard was out of touch with reality. Apparently his agricultural and sociological works are a solid meal of hard-won facts and of conclusions firmly drawn. When he decided that the only hope for the land lay in a scheme which flouted all his political preferences and shattered all his treasured hopes for his own class and his own family, he recommended that scheme without flinching.

Here lies the true greatness of the man; what Mr Cohen calls his 'overall sturdiness'. Even as an author he can sometimes be shrewd—as when in *She* Allan Quatermain neither succumbs to the charms of Ayesha nor believes her 'tall' autobiographical stories. By making Quatermain keep his head Haggard shows that he can keep his own.

But though Haggard had sense, he was ludicrously unaware of his limitations. He attempts to philosophise. Again and again in his stories we see a commonplace intelligence, armed (or hampered) with an eclectic outfit of vaguely Christian, theosophical and spiritualistic notions, trying to say something profound about that fatal subject, 'Life'. This is seen at its embarrassing worst whenever Ayesha speaks. If she was really Wisdom's daughter, she did not take after her parent. Her thought is of the regrettable type called 'Higher'.

What keeps us reading in spite of all these defects is of course the story itself, the myth. Haggard is the text-book case of the mythopoeic gift pure and simple—isolated, as if for inspection, from nearly all those more specifically literary powers with which it so fortunately co-exists in, say, *The Ancient Mariner, Dr Jekyll and Mr Hyde*, or *The Lord of the Rings*. To make matters even clearer, in Haggard himself the mythopoeic power seems to have grown less as the literary art improved. *Ayesha* is not such good myth as *She*, but it is better written.

This gift, when it exists in full measure, is irresistible. We can say of this, as Aristotle said of metaphor, 'no man can learn it from another'. It is the work of what Kipling called 'the daemon'. It triumphs over all obstacles and makes us tolerate all faults. It is quite unaffected by any foolish notions which the author himself, after the daemon has left him, may entertain about his own myths. He knows no more about them than any other man. It was silly of Haggard to treasure a belief that there was, in a factual sense, 'something in' his myths. But we, as readers, need not concern ourselves with that at all.

The mythical status of *She* is indisputable. As we all know, Jung went to it for the embodiment of an archetype. But even Jung did not, I think, get to the centre. If his view were right, the myth ought to function only for those to whom Ayesha is a powerfully erotic image. And she is not so for all who love *She*. To myself, for example, Ayesha or any other tragedy Queen—any tall, crowned, stormy, deep-breasted contralto with thunder in her brow and lightnings in her eye—is one of the most effective anti-aphrodisiacs in the world. Ultimately the life of the myth is elsewhere.

The story of Ayesha is not an escape, but it is about escape; about an attempt at the great escape, daringly made and terribly frustrated. Its closest relative, perhaps its child, is Morris's *Well at the World's End*, which came ten years later. Both stories externalise the same psychological forces; our irreconcilable reluctance to die, our craving for an immortality in the flesh, our empirical knowledge that this is impossible, our intermittent awareness that it is not even really desirable, and (octaves deeper than all these) a very primitive feeling that the attempt, if it could be made, would be unlawful and would call down the vengeance of the gods. In both books the wild, transporting, and (we feel) forbidden hope is aroused. When fruition seems almost in sight, horrifying disaster shatters our dream. Haggard's version is better than Morris's. Morris makes his heroine too human, too wholesome. Haggard, truer to our feeling, surrounds the lonely she-Prometheus with terror and misery.

Haggard's best work will survive because it is based on an appeal well above high-water mark. The fullest tides of fashion cannot demolish it. A great myth is relevant as long as the predicament of humanity lasts; as long as humanity lasts. It will always work, on those who can receive it, the same catharsis.

Haggard will last, but so will the hatred of Haggard. The vindictiveness with which adverse critics attacked him in his own day had, no doubt, some local and temporary causes. His own truculence was one. Another was the natural jealousy of the Gigadibs who can produce only a *succès d'estime* for the writer who produces 'popular'—but also living and viable—work. The author of a *Gorboduc* always has a keen eye for the faults of a *Tamburlaine*. But there was, and there always will be, a deeper cause. No one is indifferent to the mythopoeic. You either love it or else hate it 'with a perfect hatred'.

This hatred comes in part from a reluctance to meet Archetypes; it is an involuntary witness to their disquieting vitality. Partly, it springs from an uneasy awareness that the most 'popular' fiction, if only it embodies a real myth, is so very much more serious than what is generally called 'serious' literature. For it deals with the permanent and inevitable, whereas an hour's shelling, or perhaps a ten-mile walk, or even a dose of salts, might annihilate many of the problems in which the characters of a refined and subtle novel are entangled. Read James's letters and see what happened to him for some weeks after the war broke out in 1914. He presently builds up the Jamesian world again; but for a time it seemed to have 'left not a wrack behind'.

George Orwell

Now that the rumpus about the performance of Orwell's *1984* on television is dying down, it may be opportune to raise a question which has exercised my mind for a considerable time.* Why is it that, even before the recent spate of publicity, I met ten people who knew *1984* for one who knew *Animal Farm*?

Here we have two books by the same author which deal, at bottom, with the same subject. Both are very bitter, honest and honourable recantations. They express the disillusionment of one who had been a revolutionary of the familiar, *entre guerre* pattern and had later come to see that all totalitarian rulers, however their shirts may be coloured, are equally the enemies of Man.

Since the subject concerns us all and the disillusionment has been widely shared, it is not surprising that either book, or both, should find plenty of readers, and both are obviously the works of a very considerable writer. What puzzles me is the marked preference of the public for *1984*. For it seems to me (apart from its magnificent, and fortunately detachable, Appendix on 'Newspeak') to be merely a flawed, interesting book; but the *Farm* is a work of genius which may well outlive the particular and (let us hope) temporary conditions that provoked it.

To begin with, it is very much the shorter of the two. This in itself would not, of course, show it to be the better. I am the last person to think so. Callimachus, to be sure, thought a great book a great evil, but then I think Callimachus a great prig. My

---

*An adaptation of *1984* was televised by the BBC on 12 December 1954.

appetite is hearty and when I sit down to read I like a square meal. But in this instance the shorter book seems to do all that the longer one does; and more. The longer book does not justify its greater length. There is dead wood in it. And I think we can all see where the dead wood comes.

In the nightmare State of *1984* the rulers devote a great deal of time—which means that the author and readers also have to devote a great deal of time—to a curious kind of anti-sexual propaganda. Indeed the amours of the hero and heroine seem to be at least as much a gesture of protest against that propaganda as a natural outcome of affection or appetite.

Now it is, no doubt, possible that the masters of a totalitarian State might have a bee in their bonnets about sex as about anything else; and, if so, that bee, like all their bees, would sting. But we are shown nothing in the particular tyranny Orwell has depicted which would make this particular bee at all probable. Certain outlooks and attitudes which at times introduced this bee into the Nazi bonnet are not shown at work here. Worse still, its buzzing presence in the book raises questions in all our minds which have really no very close connection with the main theme and are all the more distracting for being, in themselves, of interest.

The truth is, I take it, that the bee has drifted in from an earlier (and much less valuable) period of the author's thought. He grew up in a time of what was called (very inaccurately) 'anti-Puritanism'; when people who wanted—in Lawrence's characteristic phrase—'to do dirt on sex'* were among the stock enemies. And, wishing to blacken the villains as much as possible, he decided to fling this charge against them as well as all the relevant charges.

But the principle that any stick is good enough to beat your villain with is fatal in fiction. Many a promising 'bad character' (for example, Becky Sharp) has been spoiled by the addition of an inappropriate vice. All the passages devoted to this theme in *1984* ring false to me. I am not now complaining of what some would

---

* 'Pornography and Obscenity' in *Phoenix: The Posthumous Papers of D. H. Lawrence,* ed. Edward D. MacDonald (1936).

call (whether justly or not) a 'bad smell' in the erotic passages. At least not of bad smells in general only of the smell of red herring.

But this is only the clearest instance of the defect which, throughout, makes *1984* inferior to the *Farm*. There is too much in it of the author's own psychology: too much indulgence of what he feels as a man, not pruned or mastered by what he intends to make as an artist. The *Farm* is work of a wholly different order. Here the whole thing is projected and distanced. It becomes a myth and is allowed to speak for itself. The author shows us hateful things; he doesn't stammer or speak thick under the surge of his own hatred. The emotion no longer disables him because it has all been used, and used to make something.

One result is that the satire becomes more effective. Wit and humour (absent from the longer work) are employed with devastating effect. The great sentence 'All animals are equal but some are more equal than others' bites deeper than the whole of *1984*.

Thus the shorter book does all that the longer does. But it also does more. Paradoxically, when Orwell turns all his characters into animals he makes them more fully human. In *1984* the cruelty of the tyrants is odious, but it is not tragic; odious like a man skinning a cat alive, not tragic like the cruelty of Regan and Goneril to Lear.

Tragedy demands a certain minimum stature in the victim; and the hero and heroine of *1984* do not reach that minimum. They become interesting at all only in so far as they suffer. That is claim enouth (Heaven knows) on our sympathies in real life, but not in fiction. A central character who escapes nullity only by being tortured is a failure. And the hero and heroine in this story are surely such dull, mean little creatures that one might be introduced to them once a week for six months without even remembering them.

In *Animal Farm* all this is changed. The greed and cunning of the pigs is tragic (not merely odious) because we are made to care about all the honest, well-meaning, or even heroic beasts whom they exploit. The death of Boxer the horse moves us more than all the more elaborate cruelties of the other book. And not only moves, but convinces. Here, despite the animal disguise, we feel we are in a real world. This—this congeries of guzzling pigs, snapping dogs, and heroic horses—this is what humanity is like; very good, very bad, very pitiable, very honourable. If men were only like the people in *1984* it would hardly be worth while writing stories about them. It is as if Orwell could not see them until he put them into a beast fable.

Finally, *Animal Farm* is formally almost perfect; light, strong, balanced. There is not a sentence that does not contribute to the whole. The myth says all the author wants it to say and (equally important) it doesn't say anything else. Here is an *objet d'art* as durably satisfying as a Horatian ode or a Chippendale chair.

That is why I find the superior popularity of *1984* so discouraging. Something must, of course, be allowed for mere length. The booksellers say that short books will not sell. And there are reasons not discreditable. The weekend reader wants something that will last till Sunday evening; the traveller wants something that will last as far as Glasgow.

Again, *1984* belongs to a genre that is now more familiar than a beast-fable; I mean the genre of what may be called 'Dystopias', those nightmare visions of the future which began, perhaps, with Wells's *Time Machine* and *The Sleeper Wakes*. I would like to hope that these causes are sufficient. Certainly, it would be alarming if we had to conclude either that the use of the imagination had so decayed that readers demand in all fiction a realistic surface and cannot treat any fable as more than a 'juvenile', or else that the bed-scenes in *1984* are the flavouring without which no book can now be sold.

The Death of
Words

I think it was Miss [Rose] Macaulay who complained in one of her delightful articles (strong and light as steel wire) that the dictionaries are always telling us of words 'now used only in a bad sense'; seldom or never of words 'now used only in a good sense'. It is certainly true that nearly all our terms of abuse were originally terms of description; to call a man *villain* defined his legal status long before it came to denounce his morality. The human race does not seem contented with the plain dyslogistic words. Rather than say that a man is dishonest or cruel or unreliable, they insinuate that he is illegitimate, or young, or low in the social scale, or some kind of animal; that he is a 'peasant slave', a *bastard*, a *cad*, a *knave*, a *dog*, a *swine*, or (more recently) an *adolescent*.

But I doubt if that is the whole story. There are, indeed, few words which were once insulting and are now complimentary— *democrat* is the only one that comes readily to mind. But surely there are words that have become *merely* complimentary—words which once had a definable sense and which are now nothing more than noises of vague approval? The clearest example is the word *gentleman*. This was once (like *villain*) a term which defined a social and heraldic fact. The question whether Snooks was a gentleman was almost as soluble as the question whether he was a barrister or a Master of Arts. The same question, asked forty years ago (when it was asked very often), admitted of no solution. The word had become merely eulogistic, and the qualities on which the eulogy was based varied from moment to moment even in the mind of the same speaker. This is one of the ways in which words die. A skilful doctor of words will pronounce the disease to be mortal at that moment when the word in question begins to harbour the adjectival parasites *real* or *true*. As long as *gentleman* has a clear meaning, it is enough to say that So-and-so is a gentleman. When we begin saying that he is a 'real gentleman' or 'a true gentleman' or 'a gentleman in the truest sense' we may be sure that the word has not long to live.

I would venture, then, to enlarge Miss Macaulay's observation. The truth is not simply that words originally innocent tend to acquire a bad sense. The vocabulary of flattery and insult is continually enlarged at the expense of the vocabulary of definition. As old horses go to the knacker's yard, or old ships to the breakers, so words in their last decay go to swell the enormous list of synonyms for *good* and *bad*. And as long as most people are more anxious to express their likes and dislikes than to describe facts, this must remain a universal truth about language.

This process is going on very rapidly at the moment. The words *abstract* and *concrete* were first coined to express a distinction which is really necessary to thought; but it is only for the very highly educated that they still do so. In popular language *concrete* now means something like 'clearly defined and practicable'; it has become a term of praise. *Abstract* (partly under the phonetic infection of *abstruse*) means 'vague, shadowy, unsubstantial'; it has become a term of reproach. *Modern*, in the mouths of many speakers, has ceased to be a chronological term; it has 'sunk into a good sense' and often means little more than 'efficient' or (in some contexts) 'kind'; '*medieval barbarities*'; in the mouths of the same speakers, has no reference either to the Middle Ages or to those cultures classified as barbarian. It means simply 'great or wicked cruelties'. *Conventional* can no longer be used in its proper sense without explanation. *Practical* is a mere term of approval; *contemporary*, in certain schools of literary criticism, is little better.

To save any word from the eulogistic and dyslogistic abyss is a task worth the efforts of all who love the English language. And I can think of one word—the word *Christian*—which is at this moment on the brink. When politicians talk of '*Christian* moral standards' they are not always thinking of anything which distinguishes Christian morality from Confucian or Stoic or Benthamite morality. One often feels that it is merely one literary variant among the 'adorning epithets' which, in our political style, the expression 'moral standards' is felt to require; *civilised* (another ruined word) or *modern* or *democratic* or *enlightened* would have done just as well. But it will really be a great nuisance if the word *Christian* becomes simply a synonym for *good*. For historians, if no one else, will still sometimes need the word in its proper sense, and what will they do? That is always the trouble about allowing words to slip into the abyss. Once turn *swine* into a mere insult, and you need a new word (*pig*) when you want to talk about the animal. Once let *sadism* dwindle into a useless synonym for *cruelty*, and what do you do when you have to refer to the highly special perversion which actually afflicted M. de Sade?

It is important to notice that the danger to the word *Christian* comes not from its open enemies, but from its friends. It was not egalitarians, it was officious admirers of gentility, who killed the word *gentleman*. The other day I had occasion to say that certain people were not Christians; a critic asked how I dared say so, being unable (as of course I am) to read their hearts. I had used the word to mean 'persons who profess belief in the specific doctrines of Christianity'; my critic wanted me to use it in what he would (rightly) call 'a far deeper sense'—a sense so deep that no human observer can tell to whom it applies.

And is that deeper sense not more important? It is indeed; just as it was more important to be a 'real' gentleman than to have coat-armour. But the most important sense of a word is not always the most useful. What is the good of deepening a word's connotation if you deprive the word of all practicable denotation? Words, as well as women, can be 'killed with kindness'. And when, however reverently, you have killed a word you have also, as far as in you lay, blotted from the human mind the thing that word originally stood for. Men do not long continue to think what they have forgotten how to say.

The Parthenon
and the Optative

'The trouble with these boys', said a grim old classical scholar looking up from some milk-and-watery entrance papers which he had been marking: 'the trouble with these boys is that the masters have been talking to them about the Parthenon when they should have been talking to them about the Optative.' We all knew what he meant. We had read work like that ourselves.

Ever since then I have tended to use the Parthenon and the Optative as the symbols of two types of education. The one begins with hard, dry things like grammar, and dates, and prosody; and it has at least the chance of ending in a real appreciation which is equally hard and firm though not equally dry. The other begins in 'Appreciation' and ends in gush. When the first fails it has, at the very least, taught the boy what knowledge is like. He may decide that he doesn't care for knowledge; but he knows he doesn't care for it, and he knows he hasn't got it. But the other kind fails most disastrously when it most succeeds. It teaches a man to feel vaguely cultured while he remains in fact a dunce. It makes him think he is enjoying poems he can't construe. It qualifies him to review books he does not understand, and to be intellectual without intellect. It plays havoc with the very distinction between truth and error.

And yet, education of the Parthenon type is often recommended by those who have and love real learning. They are moved by a kind of false reverence for the Muses. What they value, say, in Literature, seems to them so delicate and spiritual a thing that they cannot bear to see it (as they think) degraded by such coarse, mechanic attendants as paradigms, blackboards, marks and examination papers. They point to the questions examiners set, 'Give the context of any five of the following and add any necessary explanation.' What has that to do with the real quality of *The Tempest*? Would it not be better just to teach the boys to *appreciate* it?

But there is a profound misunderstanding here. These well-meaning educationalists are quite right in thinking that literary appreciation is a delicate thing. What they do not seem to see is that for this very reason elementary examinations on literary subjects ought to confine themselves to just those dry and factual questions which are so often ridiculed. The questions were never supposed to test appreciation; the idea was to find out whether the boy had read his books. It was the reading, not the being examined, which was expected to do him good. And this, so far from being a defect in such examinations is just what renders them useful or even tolerable.

Let us take an example from a higher sphere. A plain, factual examination in Scripture is, at the very worst, a harmless affair. But who could endure an examination which tried to find out whether the candidates were 'saved' and demanded 60 per cent for a Credit Pass in Sanctity? The situation in literary subjects bears a certain analogy to this. Tell the boy to 'mug up' a book and then set questions to find out whether he has done so. At best, he may have learned (and, best of all, unconsciously) to enjoy a great poem. At second best he has done an honest piece of work and exercised his memory and reason. At worst, we have done him no harm: have not pawed and dabbled in his soul, have not taught him to be a prig or a hypocrite. But an elementary examination which attempts to assess 'the adventures of the soul among books' is a dangerous thing. What obsequious boys, if encouraged, will try to manufacture, and clever ones can ape, and shy ones will conceal, what dies at the touch of venality, is called to come forward and *perform*, to exhibit itself, at that very age when its timid, half-conscious stirrings can least endure such self-consciousness.

How easily such false reverence can defeat itself may be seen in the Norwood Report.* The makers of that Report want external examinations in English to be abolished at schools. Their reason is that literature is such a 'sensitive and elusive thing' that these examinations touch only its 'coarse fringe'. If they stopped here, though I fail to see why the coarsest part of a thing should be least touched, I might have some sympathy with them. There is a good deal to be said for excluding literature from school curricula altogether. I am not sure that the best way to make a boy love the English poets might not be to forbid him to read them and then make sure that he had plenty of opportunities to disobey you. But that is not at all what the Report intends. It wants literary appreciation to be taught. It even wants the teaching to be tested: but not by outsiders. 'The teacher's success', it says, 'can be gauged by himself or by one of his immediate colleagues who knows him well.'

Something like examination is, then, to continue. The two reforms are (*a*) that it should deal with the 'sensitive and elusive' core, instead of the 'coarse fringe' (*b*) that it must be all in the family, so to speak. The masters are to 'gauge' their own success or one another's success. I am quite at a loss to understand what we should hope from the second novelty. The whole purpose of external examinations in any subject is to get an impartial criticism from a learned outsider who can have no prejudices either about the boys or about the teachers. In direct opposition to this the Norwood Report desires as an examiner not only the teacher's colleague, but a colleague 'who knows him well'. I suppose this must be connected with the fact that the subject is 'sensitive and elusive'. But I can't, for the life of me, see how. They cannot mean that because the subject is specially unamenable to objective tests it should therefore (alone of all subjects) be tested under conditions which make objectivity ideally difficult. Mr A (just down from reading English with Dr Leavis at

---

*The Report, so called after its chairman, Sir Cyril Norwood, is entitled *Curriculum and Examinations in Secondary Schools: Report of the Committee of the Secondary School Examinations Council Appointed by the President of the Board of Education in 1941.*

Cambridge) pours out his personality—in pure non-factual Appreciation to his form. The naughty boys rag and the 'good' boys lap it all up and reproduce it. There is a result sufficiently difficult for anyone to judge objectively. But the solution is to hand judgement over to Mr B who has been living cheek by jowl with Mr A for thirteen weeks and who learned *his* kind of Appreciation from W. P. Ker at London. And meanwhile no one has found out whether the boys actually understand the words the author wrote, for that is only the 'coarse fringe'. Yet that could have been tested with tolerable accuracy by any number of people and the boys would have been spared doing spiritual gymnastics under their examiners' eyes. The old kind of examination was better.

Of course we meet many people who explain to us that they would by now have been great readers of poetry if it had not been 'spoiled for them' at school by 'doing' it for examinations of the old kind. It is theoretically possible. Perhaps they would by now have been saints if no one had ever examined them in Scripture. Perhaps they would have been strategists or heroes if they had never been put into the school O.T.C. It may be so: but why should we believe that it is. We have only their word for it; and how do *they* know?

Period
Criticism

Opening *The Listener* a few days ago I came upon an article on Chesterton by Mr James Stephens—an article which seemed to me ungenerous and even unjust.* There were two main charges made against Chesterton; the one, that he was too public (for in Mr Stephens's view poetry is a very private affair) and the other, that he was 'dated'. The first need not, perhaps, be discussed here at very great length. Mr Stephens and I find ourselves on opposite sides of a very well-known fence, and Mr Stephens's side is, I must confess, the popular one at present. It still seems to me that the burden of proof rests on those who describe as 'private' compositions which their authors take pains to have multiplied by print and which are advertised and exposed for sale in shops. It is an odd method of securing privacy. But this question can wait. It certainly would not have worried Chesterton. Nor would the maxim that any poetry which is immediately and widely accept-able (like that of Euripides, Virgil, Horace, Dante, Chaucer, Shakespeare, Dryden, Pope, and Tennyson) must be merely 'peasant' poetry have offended a man who desired nothing so much as the restoration of the peasantry. But the question of 'dating' remains.

It is very difficult here to resist turning the tables, to ask what writer smells more unmistakably of a particular period than

---

* 'The "Period Talent" of G. K. Chesterton', *The Listener* (17 October 1946).

Mr Stephens himself. That peculiar mixture of mythology and theosophy—Pan and Aengus, leprechauns and angels, re-incarnation and the sorrows of Deirdre—if this does not carry a man back into the world of Lady Gregory, AE, the middle Yeats, and even Mr Algernon Blackwood, then the word 'period' really has no meaning. Hardly any book written in our century would be so nearly dated by internal evidence as *The Crock of Gold.** Even Mr Stephens's curious suggestion that detective stories (of which Chesterton was notoriously guilty) somehow helped to produce the first German war could be retorted. It would be just as plausible to trace the Nazi ideology to the orgiastic elements in Mr. Stephens's own work; to the cult of Pan, the revolt against reason (symbolised by the Philosopher's journey, imprisonment, and rescue) or the figure of the Uglist Man. And it might easily be maintained that the theological background of Chesterton's imaginative books has dated a good deal less than the blend of Celtic Twilight and serious occultism (Yeats claimed to be a practising magician) which we cannot help surmising for Mr Stephens.

But though this would be easy it would not be worth doing. To prove that Mr Stephens had dated would not be to prove that Chesterton was perennial. And there is, for me, another reason for not answering Mr Stephens with this *argumentum ad hominem*. I still like Mr. Stephens's books. He holds in my private pantheon a place inferior to Chesterton's but quite as secure. It is inferior because the proportion of dead wood in *The Crock of Gold*, *The Demi-Gods* and *Here Are Ladies* (there is no dead wood in *Deirdre*) seems to me higher than in the *White Horse*, *The Man Who Was Thursday*, or *The Flying Inn*.† I think the long paragraphs of what used, at Boston, to be called 'Transcendentalism' which we find in Mr Stephens are bad, sometimes even nonsensical. But then they always were bad: dates have nothing to do with it. On the other hand the gigantic (and, *in the proper sense*, Rabelaisian) comic effects—the arrest of the Philosopher or the post-mortal

*James Stephens, *The Crock of Gold* (1912), *The Demi-Gods* (1914), *Here Are Ladies* (1913), *Deirdre* (1923).
†G. K. Chesterton, *The Ballad of the White Horse* (1911), *The Man Who Was Thursday* (1908), *The Flying Inn* (1914).

adventures of O'Brien and the threepenny bit—are inexhaustible. So is the character of that admirable *picaro* Patsy MacCann. So is the Ass. So is the painting of nature; the trees that stood holding their leaves tightly in the wind, or the crow that said 'I'm the devil of a crow'. I cannot give up Mr Stephens. If anyone writes a silly, spiteful article to say that Mr Stephens was only a 'period' talent, I will fight on that issue as long as there is a drop of ink in my pen.

The truth is that the whole criticism which turns on dates and periods, as if age-groups were the proper classification of readers, is confused and even vulgar. (I do not mean that Mr Stephens is vulgar. A man who is not a vulgar man may do a vulgar thing: you will find this explained in Aristotle's *Ethics*.) It is vulgar because it appeals to the desire to be up to date: a desire only fit for dressmakers. It is confused because it lumps together the different ways in which a man can be 'of his period'.

A man may be of his period in the negative sense. That is to say he may deal with things which are of no permanent interest but only seemed to be of interest because of some temporary fashion. Thus Herbert's poems in the shape of altars and crosses are 'dated'; thus, perhaps, the occultist elements in the Celtic school are 'dated'. A man is likely to become 'dated' in this way precisely because he is anxious not to be dated, to be 'contemporary': for to move with the times is, of course, to go where all times go. On the other hand a man may be 'dated' in the sense that the forms, the set-up, the paraphernalia, whereby he expresses matter of permanent interest, are those of a particular age. In that sense the greatest writers are often the most dated. No one is more unmistakably ancient Achaean than Homer, more scholastic than Dante, more feudal than Froissart, more 'Elizabethan' than Shakespeare. *The Rape of the Lock* is a perfect (and never obsolete) period piece. *The Prelude* smells of its age. *The Waste Land* has 'Twenties' stamped on every line. Even Isaiah will reveal to a careful student that it was not composed at the court of Louis XIV nor in modern Chicago.

The real question is in which sense Chesterton was of his period. Much of his work, admittedly, was ephemeral journalism: it is dated in the first sense. The little books of essays are now mainly of historical interest. Their parallel in Mr Stephens's work is not his romances but his articles in *The Listener*. But Chesterton's imaginative works seem to me to be in quite a different position. They are, of course, richly composed. The anti-Germanicism in the *Ballad of the White Horse* belongs to a silly and transitory historical heresy of Mr Belloc's—always, on the intellectual side, a disastrous influence on Chesterton. And in the romances, the sword-sticks, the hansom cabs, the anarchists, all go back both to a real London and to an imagined London (that of *The New Arabian Nights*) which have receded from us. But how is it possible not to see that what comes through all this is permanent and dateless? Does not the central theme of the *Ballad*—the highly paradoxical message which Alfred receives from the Virgin—embody the feeling, and the only possible feeling, with which in any age almost defeated men take up such arms as are left them and win? Hence in the very nadir of the late war a very different, and exquisite, poet (Miss Ruth Pitter) unconsciously and inevitably struck exactly the same note with the line:

All but divine and desperate hopes go down
and are no more.

Hence in those quaking days after the fall of France a young friend of mine (just about to enter the R.A.F.) and I found ourselves quoting to one another stanza after stanza of the *Ballad*. There was nothing else to say.

So in the stories. Read again *The Flying Inn*. Is Lord Ivywood obsolete? The doctrinaire politician, aristocratic yet revolutionary, inhuman, courageous, eloquent, turning the vilest treacheries and most abominable oppressions into periods that echo with lofty magnanimity—is this out of date? Are the withers of any modern journalist quite unwrung when he reads of Hibbs However? Or read again *The Man Who Was Thursday*. Compare it with another good writer, Kafka. Is the difference simply that the one is 'dated' and the other contemporary? Or is it rather that while both give a powerful picture of the loneliness and bewilderment which each one of us encounters in his (apparently) single-handed struggle with the universe, Chesterton, attributing to the universe a more complicated disguise, and admitting the exhilaration as well as the terror of the struggle, has got in rather more; is more balanced: in that sense, more classical, more permanent?

I will tell Mr Stephens what that man is like who can see nothing in these stories but an Edwardian 'period' piece. He is like a man who should look into Mr Stephens's *Deirdre* (the one unmistakably great and almost perfect book among its author's many good books) and having seen the names (Connohar, Deirdre, Fergus, Naoise) should mutter 'All the old Abbey Theatre stuff' and read no more. If Mr Stephens is too modest to reply that such a man would be a fool, I will do it for him. Such a man would be a very notable fool: a fool first for disliking the early Yeats; second, for assuming that any book on the same theme must be like the early Yeats; and a fool thirdly for missing some of the finest heroic narrative, some of the most disciplined pathos, and some of the cleanest prose which our century has seen.

Different Tastes
in Literature

I have been thinking once again about the troublesome problem
of differences in what is called Taste, though the implications of
the word *Taste*, if taken seriously, would leave us with no
problem. If we really thought that a man's choice between Miss
Ruby M. Ayres and Tolstoy were quite on all fours with his choice
between mild and bitter beer, we should not discuss it, or not
seriously. But, in fact, we do not really think so. We may say so,
in the heat of argument, but we don't believe it. The idea that
some preferences in art are really better than others cannot be got
rid of: and this idea, brought into conflict with the fact that there
seem to be no objective tests, engenders the problem.

Now, without supposing that I am going to solve that
problem in an article, I have been seriously wondering of late,
whether we do not make it unnecessarily difficult by an initial
mis-statement. Again and again, one finds a writer assuming at
the outset that some people like bad art in just the same way as
others like good art. This is what I question. I am going to
submit that, in a certain recognisable sense, bad art never
succeeds with anyone.

But I must first explain what I mean by bad art. If by bad art
you mean, say, *The Niblung's Ring, Marmion* and Sullivan, then
admittedly the theory I am going to advance will not work. You
must pitch your standard a good deal lower than that. You must
mean by bad art the things which are not even considered among

people who discuss the question seriously at all, but which blare from every radio, pour from every circulating library, and hang on the wall of every hotel. The mis-statement I am attacking is the statement that *those* things are, by some people, enjoyed as much as good art is enjoyed by others—things like the poetry of Miss Ella Wheeler Wilcox or the latest popular hit in music. I would include certain posters but by no means all.

There is, of course, no doubt that these things are liked *in some way*. The wireless is turned on, the novels circulate, the poems are bought. But have we evidence that they fill in anyone's life the place that good art fills in the lives of those who love it? Look at the man who enjoys bad music, while he is enjoying it. His appetite is indeed hearty. He is prepared to hear his favourite any number of times a day. But he does not necessarily stop talking while it is going on. He joins in. He whistles, beats time with his feet, dances round the room, or uses his cigarette or mug as a conductor's baton. And when it is over, or before it is over, he will be talking to you about something else. I mean when the actual performance is over; when it is 'over' in another sense, when that song or dance has gone out of fashion, he never thinks of it again except perhaps as a curiosity.

In literature the characteristics of the 'consumer' of bad art are even easier to define. He (or she) may want her weekly ration of fiction very badly indeed, may be miserable if denied it. But he never re-reads. There is no clearer distinction between the literary and the unliterary. It is infallible. The literary man re-reads, other men simply read. A novel once read is to them like yesterday's newspaper. One may have some hopes of a man who has never read the *Odyssey*, or Malory, or Boswell, or *Pickwick*: but none (as regards literature) of the man who tells you he *has* read them, and thinks that settles the matter. It is as if a man said he had once washed, or once slept, or once kissed his wife, or once gone for a walk. Whether the bad poetry is re-read or not (it gravitates suspiciously towards the spare bedroom) I do not know. But the very fact that we do not know is significant. It does not creep into the conversation of those who buy it. One never finds two of its lovers capping quotations and settling down to a good evening's talk about their favourite. So with the bad picture. The purchaser says, no doubt sincerely, that he finds it lovely, sweet, beautiful, charming or (more probably) 'nice'. But he hangs it where it cannot be seen and never looks at it again.

In all this, surely, we find the symptoms of a real want for bad art, but of a want which is not even in the same species with men's want for good art. What the patrons of the bad art clearly desire—and get—is a pleasant background to life, a something that will fill up odd moments, 'packing' for the mental trunk or 'roughage' for the mental stomach. There is really no question of *joy*: of an experience with a razor's edge which re-makes the whole mind, which produces 'the holy spectral shiver', which can make a man (as the 'wind musique' made Pepys) feel 'really sick—just as I have formerly been when in love with my wife'. The pleasure in bad art is not an occurrence, in unfortunate context, of the same pleasure men take in good art. The desire for bad art is the desire bred of habit: like the smoker's desire for tobacco, more marked by the extreme *malaise* of denial than by any very strong delight in fruition.

Hence, one's first experiences of real joy in the arts did not appear as rivals to one's previous humdrum pleasures. When as a boy I passed from *Lays of Ancient Rome* (which are not nearly bad enough to make the point clear, but will have to serve—my father's shelves were deficient in really bad books) to *Sohrab and Rustum*, I did not in the least feel that I was getting in more quantity or better quality a pleasure I had already known. It was more as if a cupboard which one had hitherto valued as a place for hanging coats proved one day, when you opened the door, to lead to the garden of the Hesperides: as if a food one had enjoyed for the taste proved one day to enable you (like dragon's blood) to understand the speech of birds: as if water, besides quenching your thirst, suddenly became an intoxicant. One discovered that the old, familiar phenomenon 'Poetry' could be used, insisted on being used, for a wholly new purpose. Such transitions are simply misrepresented by saying 'the boy began to like poetry', or 'began to like better poetry'. What really happens is that something which has lain in the background as one of the minor pleasures of life—not radically different from toffee—leaps forward and envelopes you till you are (in Pepys's sense) 'really sick', till you tremble and grow hot and cold like a lover.

I suspect, therefore, that we must never say, simply, that some men like good art and some men like bad. The error here lurks in the verb *like*. You might as well infer from the French uses of *aimer* that a man 'loves' a woman as he 'loves' golf and start trying to compare these two 'loves' in terms of better and worse 'taste'. We have, in fact, been the victims of a pun. The proper statement is that some men like bad art: but that good art produces a response for which 'liking' is the wrong word. And this other response has, perhaps, never been produced in anyone by bad art.

Never? Are there not books which produced in us the very ecstasy I have described (in youth) and which we now judge to be bad? There are two answers. In the first place, if the theory I am suggesting works for most cases, it is worth considering whether the apparent exceptions may not be only apparent. Perhaps any book which has really excoriated any reader, however young, has some real good in it, and secondly—but that, I must postpone till next week.

I was suggesting last week that bad art is never really enjoyed in the same sense in which good art is enjoyed. It is only 'liked': it never startles, prostrates, and takes captive. Now if I say that, I come up against a difficulty. It has never been better put than by that fine and neglected artist, Mr Forrest Reid. In the little autobiography called *Apostate* he describes his delight, as a boy, in Miss Marie Corelli's *Ardath*. Even at that age the last part seemed to him 'so bad that it weakened the impression of what had gone before'. But that earlier impression remained. Perhaps wisely Mr Reid has not risked an adult re-reading. He has feared that 'its gorgeousness would all too likely strike me as vulgarity, its passionate adventure as melodrama, its poetry as a crude straining after effect'. But none the less, adds Mr Reid (who is as little likely as any man alive to be deceived in such a matter), there is no use in 'pretending that the old pleasure was not an aesthetic pleasure at all. It was. That is the whole point', and he contributes the important suggestion: 'What I got then probably was the *Ardath* of Miss Corelli's imagination; what I should get now would be the very much less splendid *Ardath* of her actual achievement.'

This diagnosis may not be correct. Mr Reid may have got the *Ardath* of the author's imagination, or he may have got the *Ardath* of his own: that is, he may really have been enjoying an embryonic composition of his own stimulated by mere hints in the book. But it is not necessary to decide between these two possibilities. The point is that, on either view, he was enjoying the book not for what it really was but for what it was not. And this sort of thing very often happens when the reader is imaginatively superior to the author, and is also young and uncritical. Thus for a boy in the first bloom of his imagination the crudest picture of a galleon under sail may do all that is necessary. Indeed he hardly *sees* the picture at all. At the first hint he is a thousand miles away, the brine is on his lips, her head rising and falling, and gulls have come to show that undiscovered country is near.

What I will not admit is that this overthrows, in general, the principle that bad art never enraptures. It may overthrow the ready application of that principle as a measuring rod. So much the better. We want to be sure that there is a real distinction between good and bad, that what we call advances in our own taste are not mere valueless fluctuations. It is not equally necessary, it may not even be desirable, that we should know with certainty, in any particular instance, who is wrong and who is right. Now the existence of mirages (such as that which, for Mr Reid, did not result from but *rested on* the words of Miss Corelli) does not overthrow the principle. In the mirage we enjoy what is not there—what we are making for ourselves or, it may be, remembering from other and better works of which the work before us is a reminder. And this is something quite distinct from the great mass of 'liking' or 'appreciation' for bad art. The patrons of sentimental poetry, bad novels, bad pictures, and merely catchy tunes are usually enjoying precisely what is there. And their enjoyment, as I have argued, is not in any way comparable to the enjoyment that other people derive from good art.

It is tepid, trivial, marginal, habitual. It does not *trouble* them, nor haunt them. To call it, and a man's rapture in great tragedy or exquisite music, by the same name, enjoyment, is little more than a pun. I still maintain that what enraptures and transports is always good. In the mirages, this good thing is not where we suppose it to be, namely, in the book or picture. But it may be good in itself—just as an oasis is a good thing though it exists a hundred miles away and not, as the desert traveller sees it, in the next valley. We have still no evidence that the qualities really present in bad art can do for anyone what good art does for some. Not because bad art gives pleasure, but because it gives a wholly different kind. Let us not be sidetracked by asking whether the distinction is between 'aesthetic' pleasure and some other kind. By certain philosophical definitions both are probably aesthetic. The point is that no one *cares* about bad art in the same way as some care about good.

If this is so then we are not really presented with rival experiences in art between which we have to choose in order to 'form a good taste'—or not on the level which I am considering. Beyond that level, when we have eliminated what is admitted to be bad by everyone who criticises at all, the critical problem may break out. You may decide that Berlioz is inferior to Bach or Shelley to Crashaw. But I suggest that any work which has ever produced intense and ecstatic delight in anyone—which has ever really *mattered*—has got inside the ring fence, and that most of what we call 'popular' art has never been a candidate for entry. It was not trying to do that: its patrons didn't want it to do that: had never conceived that art could do that or was meant to.

The criterion of good art would on this view be purely empirical. There is no external test: but there is also no mistaking it. And I would go further. I would suggest that the subtler critical discriminations—the ones that only begin inside the ring fence—always (and quite rightly) involve more than aesthetic criteria. Thus you tell me that what I experienced on first hearing the Prelude to *Parsifal* was inferior to what you experience in hearing Bach's Passion Music. I am sure you are right. But I do not think you mean, or ought to mean, that Wagner is bad art in the sense in which much popular music is bad art. It is inside the ring fence. The musical comedy tunes which I hummed as a boy were not valued by me in the same *sort* of way as *Parsifal*. There was never any possibility of competition. And when you go on to call Wagner 'bad' (in a much higher and subtler sense) you always bring in what are really either technical or moral considerations— the latter, in artistic circles, being often veiled from those who use them. Thus you condemn the Wagner as banal, or obvious, or facile (which are technical), or as vulgar, or sensual, or barbarous (which are moral). And I think you proceed quite rightly. I only plead that none of these criteria is needed, or is ever in fact used, in our preliminary distinction between 'real' or 'good' or 'serious' art and what is obviously 'bad' or (merely) 'popular' art. This was never a competitor. Wagner is 'good' by the mere fact that he can become the most important thing in life to a boy for a whole year or more. After that, decide as you please. 'Goodness' in the sense which I am referring to is established.

Some muddled people cannot understand how an axiom (say, that about things which are equal to the same thing) can be known to be true. It could not if the mind found, on this subject, any alternative proposition. But there is no alternative proposition: there is a sentence which looks (grammatically) like a proposition but is not one—for if you pronounce it nothing happens in your mind. In the same way, there is no experience alternative to that of good art. The experiences offered by bad art are not of the same sort. The world is not full of people who get out of *The Monarch of the Glen* what you get out of Tintoretto, any more than it is full of people who get drunk on water. I might as well suppose that the transitory flicker of curiosity with which I pause, passing a cricket field, to see the next ball bowled is the same as the delirious interest of a crowd at a football match.

On Criticism

I want to talk about the ways in which an author who is also a critic may improve himself as a critic by reading the criticism of his own work. But I must narrow my subject a little further. It used to be supposed that one of the functions of a critic was to help authors to write better. His praise and censure were supposed to show them where and how they had succeeded or failed, so that next time, having profited by the diagnosis, they might cure their faults and increase their virtues. That was what Pope had in mind when he said, 'Make use of every friend—and every foe.' But that is not at all what I want to discuss. In that way the author-critic might no doubt profit, as a critic, by reviews of his critical work. I am considering how he could profit, as a critic, by reviews of his non-critical works: his poems, plays, stories, or what not; what he can learn about the art of criticism by seeing it practised on himself; how he can become a better, or less bad, critic of other men's imaginative works from the treatment of his own imaginative works. For I am going to contend that when your own work is being criticised you are, in one sense, in a specially advantageous position for detecting the goodness or badness of the critique.

This may sound paradoxical, but of course all turns on my reservation, *in one sense*. There is of course another sense in which the author of a book is of all men least qualified to judge the reviews of it. Obviously he cannot judge their evaluation of it, because he is not impartial. And whether this leads him, naïvely, to hail all laudatory criticism as good and damn all unfavourable criticism as bad, or whether (which is just as likely) it leads him, in the effort against that obvious bias, to lean over backwards till he under-rates all who praise and admires all who censure him, it is equally a disturbing factor. Hence, if by criticism, you mean solely valuation, no man can judge critiques of his own work. In fact, however, most of what we call critical writing contains quite a lot of things besides evaluation. This is specially so both of reviews and of the criticism contained in literary history: for both these always should, and usually try to, inform their readers as well as direct their judgement. Now insofar as his reviewers do that, I contend that the author can see the defects and merits of their work better than anyone else. And if he is also a critic I think he can learn from them to avoid the one and emulate the other; how not to make about dead authors' books the same mistakes that have been made about his own.

I hope it will now be clear that in talking about what I think I have learned from my own critics I am not in any sense attempting what might be called an 'answer to critics'. That would, indeed, be quite incompatible with what I am actually doing. Some of the reviews I find most guilty of the critical vices I am going to mention were wholly favourable; one of the severest I ever had appeared to me wholly free from them. I expect every author has had the same experience. Authors no doubt suffer from self-love, but it need not always be voracious to the degree that abolishes all discrimination. I think fatuous praise from a manifest fool may hurt more than any depreciation.

One critical fault I must get out of the way at once because it forms no part of my real theme: I mean dishonesty. Strict honesty is not, so far as I can see, even envisaged as an ideal in the modern literary world. When I was a young, unknown writer on the eve of my first publication, a kind friend said to me, 'Will you have any difficulty about reviews? I could mention you to a few people....' It is almost as if one said to an undergraduate on the eve of a Tripos, 'Do you know any of the examiners? I could put in a word for you.' Years later another man who had reviewed me with modest favour wrote to me (though a stranger) a letter in which he said that he had really thought much more highly of my book than the review showed: 'But of course,' he said, 'if I'd praised it any more the So-and-So would not have printed me at all.' Another time someone had attacked me in a paper called X. Then he wrote a book himself. The editor of X immediately offered it to me, of all people, to review. Probably he only wanted to set us both by the ears for the amusement of the public and the increase of his sales. But even if we take the more favourable possibility—if we assume that this editor had a sort of rough idea of what they call sportsmanship, and said, 'A has gone for B, it's only fair to let B have a go at A'—it is only too plain that he has no idea of honesty towards the public out of whom he makes his living. They are entitled, at the very least, to honest, that is, to impartial, unbiased criticism: and he cannot have thought that I was the most likely person to judge this book impartially. What is even more distressing is that whenever I tell this story someone replies—mildly, unemphatically—with the question, 'And did you?' This seems to me insulting, because I cannot see how an honest man could do anything but what I did: refuse the editor's highly improper proposal. Of course they didn't mean it as an insult. That is just the trouble. When a man assumes my knavery with the intention of insulting me, it may not matter much. He may only be angry. It is when he assumes it without the slightest notion that anyone could be offended, when he reveals thus lightly his ignorance that there ever were any standards by which it could be insulting, that a chasm seems to open at one's feet.

If I exclude this matter of honesty from my main subject it is not because I think it unimportant. I think it very important indeed. If there should ever come a time when honesty in reviewers is taken for granted, I think men will look back on the present state of affairs as we now look on countries or periods in which judges or examiners commonly take bribes. My reason for dismissing the matter briefly is that I want to talk about the things I hope I have learned from my own reviewers, and this is not one of them. I had been told long before I became an author that one mustn't tell lies (not even by *suppressio veri* and *suggestio falsi*) and that we mustn't take money for doing a thing and then secretly do something quite different. I may add before leaving the point that one mustn't judge these corrupt reviewers too harshly. Much is to be forgiven to a man in a corrupt profession at a corrupt period. The judge who takes bribes in a time or place where all take bribes may, no doubt, be blamed: but not so much as a judge who had done so in a healthier civilisation.

I now turn to my main subject.

The first thing I have learned from my reviewers is, not the necessity (we would all grant that in principle) but the extreme rarity of conscientiousness in that preliminary work which all criticism should presuppose. I mean, of course, a careful reading of what one criticises. This may seem too obvious to dwell on. I put it first precisely because it is so obvious and also because I hope it will illustrate my thesis that in certain ways (not of course in others) the author is not the worst, but the best, judge of his critics. Ignorant as he may be of his book's value, he is at least an expert on its content. When you have planned and written and re-written the thing and read it twice or more in proof, you do know what is in it better than anyone else. I don't mean 'what is in it' in any subtle or metaphorical sense (there may, in that sense, be 'nothing in it') but simply what words are, and are not, printed on those pages. Unless you have been often reviewed you will hardly believe how few reviewers have really done their Prep. And not only hostile reviewers. For them one has some sympathy. To have to read an author who affects one like a bad smell or a toothache is hard work. Who can wonder if a busy man skimps this disagreeable task in order to get on as soon as possible to the far more agreeable exercise of insult and denigration. Yet we examiners do wade through the dullest, most loathsome, most illegible answers before we give a mark; not because we like it, not even because we think the answer is worth it, but because this is the thing we have accepted pay for doing. In fact, however, laudatory critics often show an equal ignorance of the text. They too had rather write than read. Sometimes, in both sorts of review, the ignorance is not due to idleness. A great many people start by thinking they know what you will say, and honestly believe they have read what they expected to read. But for whatever reason, it is certainly the case that if you are often reviewed you will find yourself repeatedly blamed and praised for saying what you never said and for not saying what you have said.

Now of course it is true that a good critic may form a correct estimate of a book without reading every word of it. That perhaps is what Sidney Smith meant when he said 'You should never read a book before you review it. It will only prejudice you.' I am not, however, speaking of evaluations based on an imperfect reading, but of direct factual falsehoods about what it contains or does not contain. Negative statements are of course particularly dangerous for the lazy or hurried reviewer. And here, at once, is a lesson for us all as critics. One passage out of the whole *Faerie Queene* will justify you in saying that Spenser sometimes does so-and-so: only an exhaustive reading and an unerring memory will justify the statement that he never does so. This everyone sees. What more easily escapes one is the concealed negative in statements apparently positive: for example in any statement that contains the predicate 'new'. One says lightly that something which Donne or Sterne or Hopkins did was new: thus committing oneself to the negative that no one had done it before. But this is beyond one's knowledge; taken rigorously, it is beyond anyone's knowledge. Again, things we are all apt to say about the growth or development of a poet may often imply the negative that he wrote nothing except what has come down to us—which no one knows. We have not seen the contents of his waste paper basket. If we had, what now looks like an abrupt change in his manner from poem A to poem B might turn out not to have been abrupt at all.

It would be wrong to leave this point without saying that, however it may be with reviewers, academic critics seem to me now better than they ever were before. The days when Macaulay could get away with the idea that the *Faerie Queene* contained the death of the Blatant Beast, or Dryden with the remark that Chapman translated the *Iliad* in Alexandrines, are over. On the whole we now do our homework pretty well. But not yet perfectly. About the more obscure works ideas still circulate from one critic to another which have obviously not been verified by actual reading. I have an amusing piece of private evidence in my possession. My copy of a certain voluminous poet formerly belonged to a great scholar. At first I thought I had found a treasure. The first and second pages were richly, and most learnedly annotated in a neat, legible hand. There were fewer on the third; after that, for the rest of the first poem, there was nothing. Each work was in the same state: the first few pages annotated, the rest in mint condition. 'Thus far into the bowels of the land' each time, and no further. Yet he had written on these works.

That, then, is the first lesson the reviewers taught me. There is, of course, another lesson in it. Let no one try to make a living by becoming a reviewer except as a last resource. This fatal ignorance of the text is not always the fruit of laziness or malice. It may be mere defeat by an intolerable burden. To live night and day with that hopeless mountain of new books (mostly uncongenial) piling up on your desk, to be compelled to say something where you have nothing to say, to be always behind-hand—indeed much is to be excused to one so enslaved. But of course to say that a thing is excusable is to confess that it needs excuse.

I now turn to something which interests me much more because the bottom sin I detect in the reviewers is one which I believe we shall all find it very difficult to banish from our own critical work. Nearly all critics are prone to imagine that they know a great many facts relevant to a book which in reality they don't know. The author inevitably perceives their ignorance because he (often he alone) knows the real facts. This critical vice may take many different forms.

1. Nearly all reviewers assume that your books were written in the same order in which they were published and all shortly before publication. There was a very good instance of this lately in the reviews of Tolkien's *Lord of the Rings*. Most critics assumed (this illustrates a different vice) that it must be a political allegory and a good many thought that the master Ring must 'be' the atomic bomb. Anyone who knew the real history of the composition knew that this was not only erroneous, but impossible; chronologically impossible. Others assumed that the mythology of his romance had grown out of his children's story *The Hobbit*. This, again, he and his friends knew to be mainly false. Now of course nobody blames the critics for not knowing these things:

how should they? The trouble is that they don't know they don't
know. A guess leaps into their minds and they write it down
without even noticing that it is a guess. Here certainly the
warning to us all as critics is very clear and alarming. Critics of
Piers Plowman and the *Faerie Queene* make gigantic constructions
about the history of these compositions. Of course, we should all
admit such constructions to be conjectural. And as conjectures,
you may ask, are they not, some of them, probable? Perhaps they
are. But the experience of being reviewed has lowered my
estimate of their probability. Because, when you start by knowing
the facts, you find that the constructions are very often wholly
wrong. Apparently the chances of their being right are low, even
when they are made along quite sensible lines. Of course I am not
forgetting that the reviewer has (quite rightly) devoted less study
to my book than the scholar has devoted to Langland or Spenser.
But I should have expected that to be compensated for by other
advantages which he has and the scholar lacks. After all, he lives
in the same period as I, subjected to the same currents of taste and
opinion, and has undergone the same kind of education. He can
hardly help knowing—reviewers are good at this sort of thing and
take an interest in it—quite a lot about my generation, my
period, and the circles in which I probably move. He and I may
even have common acquaintances. Surely he is at least as well
placed for guessing about me as any scholar is for guessing about
the dead. Yet he seldom guesses right. Hence I cannot resist the
conviction that similar guesses about the dead seem plausible
only because the dead are not there to refute them; that five
minutes' conversation with the real Spenser or the real Langland
might blow the whole laborious fabric into smithereens. And
notice that in all these conjectures the reviewer's error has been
quite gratuitous. He has been neglecting the thing he is paid to
do, and perhaps could do, in order to do something different. His
business was to give information about the book and to pass
judgement on it. These guesses about its history are quite beside
the mark. And on this point, I feel pretty sure that I write
without bias. The imaginary histories written about my books are
by no means always offensive. Sometimes they are even complimentary. There is nothing against them except that they're not

true, and would be rather irrelevant if they were. *Mutato nomine de me*. I must learn not to do the like about the dead: and if I hazard a conjecture, it must be with full knowledge, and with a clear warning to my readers, that it is a long shot, far more likely to be wrong than right.

2. Another type of critic who speculates about the genesis of your book is the amateur psychologist. He has a Freudian theory of literature and claims to know all about your inhibitions. He knows what unacknowledged wishes you were gratifying. And here of course one cannot, in the same sense as before, claim to start by knowing all the facts. By definition you are unconscious of the things he professes to discover. Therefore the more loudly you disclaim them, the more right he must be: though, oddly enough, if you admitted them, that would prove him right too. And there is a further difficulty: one is not here so free from bias, for this procedure is almost entirely confined to hostile reviewers. And now that I come to think of it, I have seldom seen it practised on a dead author except by a scholar who intended, in some measure, to debunk him. That in itself is perhaps significant. And it would not be unreasonable to point out that the evidence on which such amateur psychologists base their diagnosis would not be thought sufficient by a professional. They have not had their author on the sofa, nor heard his dreams, and had the whole case-history. But I am here concerned only with what the author can say about such reviews solely because he is the author. And surely, however ignorant he is of his unconscious, he knows something more than they about the content of his conscious mind. And he will find them wholly overlooking the (to him) perfectly obvious conscious motive for some things. If they mentioned this and then discounted it as the author's (or patient's) 'rationalisation', they might be right. But it is clear that they never thought of it. They have never seen why, from the very structure of your story, from the very nature of story telling in general, that episode or image (or something like it) had to come in at that point. It is in fact quite clear that there is one impulse in your mind of which, with all their psychology, they have never reckoned: the plastic impulse, the impulse to make a thing, to shape, to give unity, relief, contrast, pattern. But this, unhappily,

is the impulse which chiefly caused the book to be written at all. They have, clearly, no such impulse themselves, and they do not suspect it in others. They seem to fancy that a book trickles out of one like a sigh or a tear or automatic writing. It may well be that there is much in every book which comes from the unconscious. But when it is your own book you know the conscious motives as well. You may be wrong in thinking that these often give the full explanation of this or that. But you can hardly believe accounts of the sea-bottom given by those who are blind to the most obvious objects on the surface. They could be right only by accident. And I, if I attempt any similar diagnosis about the dead, shall equally be right, if at all, only by accident.

The truth is that a very large part of what comes up from the unconscious and which, for that very reason, seems so attractive and important in the early stages of planning a book, is weeded out and jettisoned long before the job is done: just as people (if they are not bores) tell us of their dreams only those which are amusing or in some other way interesting by the standards of the waking mind.

3. I now come to the imaginary history of the book's composition in a much subtler form. Here I think critics, and of course we when we criticise, are often deceived or confused as to what they are really doing. The deception may lurk in the words themselves. You and I might condemn a passage in a book for being 'laboured'. Do we mean by this that it sounds laboured? Or are we advancing the theory that it was in fact laboured? Or are we sometimes not quite sure which we mean? If we mean the second, notice that we are ceasing to write criticism. Instead of pointing out the faults in the passage we are inventing a story to explain, causally, how it came to have those faults. And if we are not careful we may complete our story and pass on as if we had done all that was necessary, without noticing that we have never even specified the faults at all. We explain something by causes without saying what the something is. We can do the same when we think we are praising. We may say that a passage is unforced or spontaneous. Do we mean that it sounds as if it were, or that it actually was written effortlessly and *currente calamo*? And whichever we mean, would it not be more interesting and more within

the critics' province to point out, instead, those merits in the passage which made us want to praise it at all?

The trouble is that certain critical terms—*inspired, perfunctory, painstaking, conventional*—imply a supposed history of composition. The critical vice I am talking about consists in yielding to the temptation they hold out and then, instead of telling us what is good and bad in a book, inventing stories about the process which led to the goodness and badness. Or are they misled by the double sense of the word *Why?* For of course the question 'Why is this bad?' may mean two things: (*a*) What do you mean by calling it bad? Wherein does its badness consist? Give me the Formal Cause. (*b*) How did it become bad? Why did he write so ill? Give me the Efficient Cause. The first seems to me the essentially critical question. The critics I am thinking of answer the second, and usually answer it wrong, and unfortunately regard this as a substitute for the answer to the first.

Thus a critic will say of a passage, 'This is an afterthought.' He is just as likely to be wrong as right. He may be quite right in thinking it bad. And he must presumably think he has discerned in it the sort of badness which one might expect to occur in an afterthought. Surely an exposure of that badness itself would be far better than an hypothesis about its origin? Certainly this is the only thing that would make the critique at all useful to the author. I as author may know that the passage diagnosed as an afterthought was in reality the seed from which the whole book grew. I should very much like to be shown what inconsistency or irrelevance or flatness makes it look like an afterthought. It might help me to avoid these errors next time. Simply to know what the critic imagines, and imagines wrongly, about the history of the passage is of no use. Nor is it of much use to the public. They have every right to be told of the faults in my book. But this fault, as distinct from a hypothesis (boldly asserted as fact) about its origin, is just what they do not learn.

Here is an example which is specially important because I am quite sure the judgement which the critic was really making was correct. In a book of essays of mine the critic said that one essay was written without conviction, was task-work, or that my heart was not in it, or something like that. Now this in itself was plumb-wrong. Of all the pieces in the book it was the one I most cared about and wrote with most ardour.* Where the critic was right was in thinking it the worst. Everyone agrees with him about that. I agree with him. But you see that neither the public nor I learns anything about that badness from his criticism. He is like a doctor who makes no diagnosis and prescribes no cure but tells you how the patient got the disease (still unspecified) and tells you wrong because he is describing scenes and events on which he has no evidence. The fond parents ask, 'What is it? Is it scarlatina or measles or chicken-pox?' The doctor replies, 'Depend upon it, he picked it up in one of those crowded trains.' (The patient actually has not travelled by train lately.) They then ask, 'But what are we to do? How are we to treat him?' The doctor replies, 'You may be quite sure it was an infection.' Then he climbs into his car and drives away.

Notice here again the total disregard of writing as a skill, the assumption that the writer's psychological state always flows unimpeded and undisguised into the product. How can they not know that in writing as in carpentry or tennis-playing or prayer or love-making or cookery or administration or anything else there is both skill and also those temporary heightenings and lowerings of skill which a man describes by saying that he is in good or bad form, that his hand is 'in' or 'out', that this is one of his good days or his bad days?

Such is the lesson, but it is very difficult to apply. It needs great perseverance to force oneself, in one's own criticism, to attend always to the product before one instead of writing fiction about the author's state of mind or methods of work: to which of course one has no direct access. 'Sincere', for example, is a word we should avoid. The real question is what makes a thing *sound* sincere or not. Anyone who has censored letters in the army must know that semi-literate people, though not in reality less sincere than others, very seldom *sound* sincere when they use the written word. Indeed we all know from our own experience in writing letters of condolence that the occasions on which we really feel

---

*Lewis, I am quite certain, is talking about the essay on William Morris in his *Selected Literary Essays* (1969).

most are not necessarily those on which our letters would suggest this. Another day, when we felt far less, our letter may have been more convincing. And of course the danger of error is greater in proportion as our own experience in the form we are criticising is less. When we are criticising a kind of work we have never attempted ourselves, we must realise that we do not know how such things are written and what is difficult or easy to do in them and how particular faults are likely to occur. Many critics quite clearly have an idea of how they think they would proceed if they tried to write the sort of book you have written, and assume that you were doing that. They often reveal unconsciously why they never have written a book of that kind.

I don't mean at all that we must never criticise work of a kind we have never done. On the contrary we must do nothing but criticise it. We may analyse and weigh its virtues and defects. What we must not do is to write imaginary histories. I know that all beer in railway refreshment rooms is bad and I could to some extent say 'why' (in one sense of the word: that is, I could give the Formal Cause)—it is tepid, sour, cloudy, and weak. But to tell you 'why' in the other sense (the Efficient Cause) I should need to have been a brewer or a publican or both and to know how beer should be brewed and kept and handled.

I would gladly be no more austere than is necessary. I must admit that words which seem, in their literal sense, to imply a history of the composition may sometimes be used as merely elliptical pointers to the character of the work done. When a man says that something is 'forced' or 'effortless' he may not really be claiming to know how it was written but only indicating in a kind of short-hand a quality he supposes everyone will recognise. And perhaps to banish all expression of this kind from our criticism would be a counsel of perfection. But I am increasingly convinced of their danger. If we use them at all, we must do so with extreme caution. We must make it quite clear to ourselves and to our readers that we do not know and are not pretending to know how things were written. Nor would it be relevant if we did. What sounds forced would be no better if it had been dashed off without pains; what sounds inspired, no worse if it had been arduously put together *invita Minerva*.

I now turn to interpretation. Here of course all critics, and we among them, will make mistakes. Such mistakes are far more venial than the sort I have been describing, for they are not gratuitous. The one sort arise when the critic writes fiction instead of criticism; the other, in the discharge of a proper function. At least I assume that critics ought to interpret, ought to try to find out the meaning or intention of a book. When they fail the fault may lie with them or with the author or with both.

I have said vaguely 'meaning' or 'intention'. We shall have to give each word a fairly definite sense. It is the author who *intends*; the book *means*. The author's intention is that which, if it is realised, will in his eyes constitute success. If all or most readers, or such readers as he chiefly desires, laugh at a passage, and he is pleased with this result, then his intention was comic, or he intended to be comic. If he is disappointed and humiliated at it, then he intended to be grave, or his intention was serious. *Meaning* is a much more difficult term. It is simplest when used of an allegorical work. In the *Romance of the Rose* plucking the rosebud means enjoying the heroine. It is still fairly easy when used of a work with a conscious and definite 'lesson' in it. *Hard Times* means, among other things, that elementary state education is bosh; *Macbeth*, that your sin will find you out; *Waverley*, that solitude and abandonment to the imagination in youth render a man an easy prey to those who wish to exploit him; the *Aeneid*, that the *res Romana* rightly demands the sacrifice of private happiness. But we are already in deep waters, for of course each of these books means a good deal more. And what are we talking about when we talk, as we do, of the 'meaning' of *Twelfth Night*, *Wuthering Heights*, or *The Brothers Karamazov*? And especially when we differ and dispute as we do, about their real or true meaning? The nearest I have yet got to a definition is something like this: the meaning of a book is the series or system of emotions, reflections, and attitudes produced by reading it. But of course this product differs with different readers. The ideally false or wrong 'meaning' would be the product in the mind of the stupidest and least sensitive and most prejudiced reader after a single careless reading. The ideally true or right 'meaning' would be that shared (in some measure) by the largest number of the best readers after repeated and careful readings over several generations, different periods, nationalities, moods, degrees of alertness, private pre-occupations, states of health, spirits, and the like cancelling one another out when (this is an important reservation) they cannot be fused so as to enrich one another. (This happens when one's readings of a work at widely different periods of one's own life, influenced by the readings that reach us indirectly through the works of critics, all modify our present reading so as to improve it.) As for the many generations, we must add a limit. These serve to enrich the perception of the meaning only so long as the cultural tradition is not lost. There may come a break or change after which readers arise whose point of view is so alien that they might as well be interpreting a new work. Medieval readings of the *Aeneid* as an allegory and Ovid as a moralist, or modern readings of the *Parlement of Foules* which make the duck and goose its heroes, would be examples. To delay, even if we cannot permanently banish such interpretations, is a large part of the function of scholarly, as distinct from pure, criticism; so doctors labour to prolong life though they know they cannot make men immortal.

Of a book's meaning, in this sense, its author is not necessarily the best, and is never a perfect, judge. One of his intentions usually was that it should have a certain meaning: he cannot be sure that it has. He cannot even be sure that the meaning he intended it to have was in every way, or even at all, better than the meaning which readers find in it. Here, therefore, the critic has great freedom to range without fear of contradiction from the author's superior knowledge.

Where he seems to me most often to go wrong is in the hasty assumption of an allegorical sense; and as reviewers make this mistake about contemporary works, so, in my opinion, scholars now often make it about old ones. I would recommend to both, and I would try to observe in my own critical practise, these principles. First, that no story can be devised by the wit of man which cannot be interpreted allegorically by the wit of some other man. The Stoic interpretations of primitive mythology, the Christian interpretations of the Old Testament, the medieval interpretations of the classics, all prove this. Therefore (2) the mere fact that you *can* allegorise the work before you is of itself no proof that it is an allegory. Of course you can allegorise it. You can allegorise anything, whether in art or real life. I think we should here take a hint from the lawyers. A man is not tried at the assizes until there has been shown to be a *prima-facie* case against him. We ought not to proceed to allegorise any work until we have plainly set out the reasons for regarding it as an allegory at all.

[Lewis, apparently, did not finish this essay for at the foot of the existing manuscript are the words:]

As regards other attributions of intention

One's own preoccupations

Quellenforschung. *Achtung*—dates

Unreal Estates

This informal conversation between Professor Lewis, Kingsley Amis, and Brian Aldiss was recorded on tape in Professor Lewis's rooms in Magdalene College a short while before illness forced him to retire. When drinks are poured, the discussion begins—

ALDISS: One thing that the three of us have in common is that we have all had stories published in the *Magazine of Fantasy and Science Fiction*, some of them pretty far-flung stories. I take it we would all agree that one of the attractions of science-fiction is that it takes us to unknown places.

AMIS: Swift, if he were writing today, would have to take us out to the planets, wouldn't he? Now that most of our *terra incognita* is—real estate.

ALDISS: There is a lot of the eighteenth-century equivalent of science-fiction which is placed in Australia or similar unreal estates.

LEWIS: Exactly: Peter Wilkins and all that. By the way, is anyone ever going to do a translation of Kepler's *Somnium*?

AMIS: Groff Conklin told me he had read the book; I think it must exist in translation. But may we talk about the worlds you created? You chose the science-fiction medium because you wanted to go to strange places? I remember with respectful and amused admiration your account of the space drive in *Out of the Silent Planet*. When Ransom and his friend get into the space-ship he says, 'How does this ship work?'

and the man says, 'It operates by using some of the lesser known properties of——' what was it?

LEWIS: Solar radiation. Ransom was reporting words without a meaning to him, which is what a layman gets when he asks for a scientific explanation. Obviously it was vague, because I'm no scientist and not interested in the purely technical side of it.

ALDISS: It's almost a quarter of a century since you wrote that first novel of the trilogy.

LEWIS: Have I been a prophet?

ALDISS: You have to a certain extent; at least, the idea of vessels propelled by solar radiation is back in favour again. Cordwiner Smith used it poetically, James Blish tried to use it technically in *The Star Dwellers*.

LEWIS: In my case it was pure mumbo-jumbo, and perhaps meant primarily to convince me.

AMIS: Obviously when one deals with isolated planets or isolated islands one does this for a certain purpose. A setting in contemporary London or a London of the future couldn't provide one with the same isolation and the heightening of consciousness it engenders.

LEWIS: The starting point of the second novel, *Perelandra*, was my mental picture of the floating islands. The whole of the rest of my labours in a sense consisted of building up a world in which floating islands could exist. And then of course the story about an averted fall developed. This is because, as you know, having got your people to this exciting country, something must happen.

AMIS: That frequently taxes people very much.

ALDISS: But I am surprised that you put it this way round. I would have thought that you constructed *Perelandra* for the didactic purpose.

LEWIS: Yes, everyone thinks that. They are quite wrong.

AMIS: If I may say a word on Professor Lewis's side, there was a didactic purpose of course; a lot of very interesting profound things were said, but—correct me if I'm wrong—I'd have thought a simple sense of wonder, extraordinary things going on, were the motive forces behind the creation.

LEWIS: Quite, but something has got to happen. The story of this averted fall came in very conveniently. Of course it wouldn't have been that particular story if I wasn't interested in those particular ideas on other grounds. But that isn't what I started from. I've never started from a message or a moral, have you?

AMIS: No, never. You get interested in the situation.

LEWIS: The story itself should force its moral upon you. You find out what the moral is by writing the story.

AMIS: Exactly: I think that sort of thing is true of all kinds of fiction.

ALDISS: But a lot of science-fiction has been written from the other point of view: those dreary sociological dramas that appear from time to time, started with a didactic purpose— to make a preconceived point—and they've got no further.

LEWIS: I suppose Gulliver started from a straight point of view? Or did it really start because he wanted to write about a lot of big and little men?

AMIS: Possibly both, as Fielding's parody of Richardson turned into *Joseph Andrews*. A lot of science-fiction loses much of the impact it could have by saying, 'Well, here we are on Mars, we all know where we are, and we're living in these pressure domes or whatever it is, and life is really very much like it is on Earth, except there is a certain climatic difference....' They accept other men's inventions rather than forge their own.

LEWIS: It's only the first journey to a new planet that is of any interest to imaginative people.

AMIS: In your reading of science-fiction have you ever come across a writer who's done this properly?

LEWIS: Well, the one you probably disapprove of because he's so very unscientific is David Lindsay, in *Voyage to Arcturus*. It's a remarkable thing, because scientifically it's nonsense, the style is appalling, and yet this ghastly vision comes through.

ALDISS: It didn't come through to me.

AMIS: Nor me. Still ... Victor Gollancz told me a very interesting remark of Lindsay's about *Arcturus*; he said, 'I shall never appeal to a large public at all, but I think that as long as our

145

civilisation lasts one person a year will read me.' I respect that attitude.

LEWIS: Quite so. Modest and becoming. I also agree with something you said in a preface, I believe it was, that some science-fiction really does deal with issues far more serious than those realistic fiction deals with; real problems about human destiny and so on. Do you remember that story about the man who meets a female monster landed from another planet with all its cubs hanging round it? It's obviously starving, and he offers them thing after thing to eat; they immediately vomit it up, until one of the young fastens on him, begins sucking his blood and immediately begins to revive. This female creature is utterly unhuman, horrible in form; there's a long moment when it looks at the man— they're in a lonely place—and then very sadly it packs up its young, and goes back into its space-ship and goes away. Well now, you could not have a more serious theme than that. What is a footling story about some pair of human lovers compared with that?

AMIS: On the debit side, you often have these marvellous large themes tackled by people who haven't got the mental or moral or stylistic equipment to take them on. A reading of more recent science-fiction shows that writers are getting more capable of tackling them. Have you read Walter Miller's *Canticle for Leibowitz*? Have you any comments on that?

LEWIS: I thought it was pretty good. I only read it once; mind you, a book's no good to me until I've read it two or three times—I'm going to read it again. It was a major work, certainly.

AMIS: What did you think about its religious feeling?

LEWIS: It came across very well. There were bits of the actual writing which one could quarrel with, but on the whole it was well imagined and well executed.

AMIS: Have you seen James Blish's novel *A Case of Conscience*? Would you agree that to write a religious novel that isn't concerned with details of ecclesiastical practice and the numbing minutiae of history and so on, science-fiction would be the natural outlet for this?

LEWIS: If you have a religion it must be cosmic; therefore it seems to me odd that this genre was so late in arriving.

ALDISS: It's been around without attracting critical attention for a long time; the magazines themselves have been going since 1926, although in the beginning they appealed mainly to the technical side. As Amis says, people have come along who can write, as well as think up engineering ideas.

LEWIS: We ought to have said earlier that that's quite a different species of science-fiction, about which I say nothing at all; those who were really interested in the technical side of it. It's obviously perfectly legitimate if it's well done.

AMIS: The purely technical and the purely imaginative overlap, don't they?

ALDISS: There are certainly the two streams, and they often overlap, for instance in Arthur Clarke's writings. It can be a rich mixture. Then there's the type of story that's not theological, but it makes a moral point. An example is the Sheckley story about Earth being blasted by radioactivity. The survivors of the human race have gone away to another planet for about a thousand years; they come back to reclaim Earth and find it full of all sorts of gaudy armour-plated creatures, vegetation, etc. One of the party says, 'We'll clear this lot out, make it habitable for man again.' But in the end the decision is, 'Well, we made a mess of the place when it was ours, let's get out and leave it to them.' This story was written about '49, when most people hadn't started thinking round the subject at all.

LEWIS: Yes, most of the earlier stories start from the opposite assumption that we, the human race, are in the right, and everything else is ogres. I may have done a little towards altering that, but the new point of view has come very much in. We've lost our confidence, so to speak.

AMIS: It's all terribly self-critical and self-contemplatory nowadays.

LEWIS: This is surely an enormous gain—a human gain, that people should be thinking that way.

AMIS: The prejudice of supposedly educated persons towards this type of fiction is fantastic. If you pick up a science-fiction magazine, particularly *Fantasy and Science-Fiction*, the range of interests appealed to and I.Q.s employed, is pretty amazing. It's time more people caught on. We've been telling them about it for some while.

LEWIS: Quite true. The world of serious fiction is very narrow.

AMIS: Too narrow if you want to deal with a broad theme. For instance, Philip Wylie in *The Disappearance* wants to deal with the difference between men and women in a general way, in twentieth-century society, unencumbered by local and temporary considerations; his point, as I understand it, is that men and women, shorn of their social roles, are really very much the same. Science-fiction, which can presuppose a major change in our environment, is the natural medium for discussing a subject of that kind. Look at the job of dissecting human nastiness carried out in Golding's *Lord of the Flies*.

LEWIS: That can't be science-fiction.

AMIS: I would dissent from that. It starts off with a characteristic bit of science-fiction situation: that World War III has begun, bombs dropped and all that....

LEWIS: Ah, well, you're now taking the German view that any romance about the future is science-fiction. I'm not sure that this is a useful classification.

AMIS: 'Science-fiction' is such a hopelessly vague label.

LEWIS: And of course a great deal of it isn't *science-* fiction. Really it's only a negative criterion: anything which is not naturalistic, which is not about what we call the real world.

ALDISS: I think we oughtn't to try to define it, because it's a self-defining thing in a way. We know where we are. You're right, though, about *Lord of the Flies*. The atmosphere is a science-fiction atmosphere.

LEWIS: It was a very terrestrial island; the best island, almost, in fiction. Its actual sensuous effect on you is terrific.

ALDISS: Indeed. But it's a laboratory case——

AMIS: —isolating certain human characteristics, to see how they would work out——

LEWIS: The only trouble is that Golding writes so well. In one of his other novels, *The Inheritors*, the detail of every sensuous impression, the light on the leaves and so on, was so good that you couldn't find out what was happening. I'd say it was almost too well done. All these little details you only notice in real life if you've got a high temperature. You couldn't see the wood for the leaves.

ALDISS: You had this in *Pincher Martin*; every feeling in the rocks, when he's washed ashore, is done with a hallucinatory vividness.

AMIS: It is, that's exactly the phrase. I think thirty years ago if you wanted to discuss a general theme you would go to the historical novel; now you would go to what I might describe in a prejudiced way as science-fiction. In science-fiction you can isolate the factors you want to examine. If you wanted to deal with the theme of colonialism, for instance, as Poul Anderson has done, you don't do it by writing a novel about Ghana or Pakistan——

LEWIS: Which involves you in such a mass of detail that you don't want to go into——

LEWIS: Would you describe Abbott's *Flatland* as science-fiction? There's so little effort to bring it into any sensuous—well, you couldn't do it, and it remains an intellectual theorem. Are you looking for an ashtray? Use the carpet.

AMIS: I was looking for the Scotch, actually.

LEWIS: Oh, yes, do, I beg your pardon.... But probably the great work in science-fiction is still to come. Futile books about the next world came before Dante, Fanny Burney came before Jane Austen, Marlowe came before Shakespeare.

AMIS: We're getting the prolegomena.

LEWIS: If only the modern highbrow critics could be induced to take it seriously ...

AMIS: Do you think they ever can?

LEWIS: No, the whole present dynasty has got to die and rot before anything can be done at all.

ALDISS: Splendid!

AMIS: What's holding them up, do you think?

LEWIS: Matthew Arnold made the horrible prophecy that literature would increasingly replace religion. It has, and it's taken on all the features of bitter persecution, great intolerance, and traffic in relics. All literature becomes a sacred text. A sacred text is always exposed to the most monstrous exegesis; hence we have the spectacle of some wretched scholar taking a pure *divertissement* written in the seventeenth century and getting the most profound ambiguities and social criticisms out of it, which of course aren't there at all....It's the discovery of the mare's nest by the pursuit of the red herring. [Laughter.] This is going to go on long after my lifetime; you may be able to see the end of it, I shan't.

AMIS: You think this is so integral a part of the Establishment that people can't overcome——

LEWIS: It's an industry, you see. What would all the people be writing *D. Phil.* theses on if this prop were removed?

AMIS: An instance of this mentality the other day: somebody referred to 'Mr Amis's I suspect rather affected enthusiasm for science-fiction....'

LEWIS: Isn't that maddening!

AMIS: You can't really like it.

LEWIS: You must be pretending to be a plain man or something....I've met the attitude again and again. You've probably reached the stage too of having theses written on yourself. I received a letter from an American examiner asking, 'Is it true that you meant this and this and this?' A writer of a thesis was attributing to me views which I have explicitly contradicted in the plainest possible English. They'd be much wiser to write about the dead, who can't answer.

ALDISS: In America, I think science-fiction is accepted on a more responsible level.

AMIS: I'm not so sure about that, you know, Brian, because when our anthology *Spectrum I* came out in the States we had less friendly and less understanding treatment from reviewers than we did over here.

LEWIS: I'm surprised at that, because in general all American reviewing is more friendly and generous than in England.

AMIS: People were patting themselves on the back in the States for not understanding what we meant.

LEWIS: This extraordinary pride in being exempt from temptations that you have not yet risen to the level of! Eunuchs boasting of their chastity! [Laughter.]

AMIS: One of my pet theories is that serious writers as yet unborn or still at school will soon regard science-fiction as a natural way of writing.

LEWIS: By the way, has any science-fiction writer yet succeeded in inventing a third sex? Apart from the third sex we all know.

AMIS: Clifford Simak invented a set-up where there were seven sexes.

LEWIS: How rare happy marriages must have been then!

ALDISS: Rather worth striving for perhaps.

LEWIS: Obviously when achieved they'd be wonderful. [Laughter.]

ALDISS: I find I would much rather write science-fiction than anything else. The dead weight is so much less there than in the field of the ordinary novel. There's a sense in which you're conquering a fresh country.

AMIS: Speaking as a supposedly realistic novelist, I've written little bits of science-fiction and this is such a tremendous liberation.

LEWIS: Well, you're a very ill-used man; you wrote a farce and everyone thought it a damning indictment of Redbrick. I've always had great sympathy for you. They will not understand that a joke is a joke. Everything must be serious.

AMIS: 'A fever chart of society.'

LEWIS: One thing in science-fiction that weighs against us very heavily is the horrible shadow of the comics.

ALDISS: I don't know about that. Titbits Romantic Library doesn't really weigh against the serious writer.

LEWIS: That's a fair analogy. All the novelettes didn't kill the ordinary legitimate novel of courtship and love.

ALDISS: There might have been a time when science-fiction and comics were weighed together and found wanting, but that at least we've got past.

AMIS: I see the comic books that my sons read, and you have there a terribly vulgar reworking of the themes that science-fiction goes in for.

LEWIS: Quite harmless, mind you. This chatter about the moral danger of the comics is absolute nonsense. The real objection is against the appalling draughtsmanship. Yet you'll find the same boy who reads them also reads Shakespeare or Spenser. Children are so terribly catholic. That's my experience with my stepchildren.

ALDISS: This is an English habit, to categorise: that if you read Shakespeare you can't read comics, that if you read science-fiction you can't be serious.

AMIS: That's the thing that annoys me.

LEWIS: Oughtn't the word *serious* to have an embargo slapped on it? 'Serious' ought to mean simply the opposite of comic, whereas now it means 'good' or 'literature' with a capital L.

ALDISS: You can be serious without being earnest.

LEWIS: Leavis demands moral earnestness; I prefer morality.

AMIS: I'm with you every time on that one.

LEWIS: I mean I'd sooner live among people who don't cheat at cards than among people who are earnest about not cheating at cards. [Laughter.]

AMIS: More Scotch?

LEWIS: Not for me, thank you, help yourself. [Liquid noises.]

AMIS: I think all this ought to stay in, you know—all these remarks about drink.

LEWIS: There's no reason why we shouldn't have a drink. Look, you want to borrow Abbott's *Flatland*, don't you? I must go to dinner, I'm afraid. [Hands over *Flatland*.] The original manuscript of the *Iliad* could not be more precious. It's only the ungodly who borroweth and payeth not again.

AMIS (READING): By A. Square.

LEWIS: But of course the word *square* hadn't the same sense then.

ALDISS: It's like the poem by Francis Thompson that ends 'She gave me tokens three, a look, a word of her winsome mouth, and a sweet wild raspberry'; there again the meaning has changed. It really was a wild raspberry in Thompson's day. [Laughter.]

LEWIS: Or the lovely one about the Bishop of Exeter, who was giving the prizes at a girls' school. They did a performance of *A Midsummer Night's Dream,* and the poor man stood up afterwards and made a speech and said [piping voice]: 'I was very interested in your delightful performance, and among other things I was very interested in seeing for the first time in my life a female Bottom.' [Guffaws.]

Books by C. S. Lewis
available from Harcourt Brace & Company
in Harvest paperback editions

All My Road Before Me: The Diary of C. S. Lewis, 1922–1927
The Business of Heaven: Daily Readings from C. S. Lewis
The Dark Tower and Other Stories
The Four Loves
Letters of C. S. Lewis
Letters to Malcolm: Chiefly on Prayer
A Mind Awake: An Anthology of C. S. Lewis
Narrative Poems
Of Other Worlds: Essays and Stories
On Stories: And Other Essays on Literature
Poems
Present Concerns
Reflections on the Psalms
Spirits in Bondage: A Cycle of Lyrics
Surprised by Joy: The Shape of My Early Life
Till We Have Faces: A Myth Retold
The World's Last Night and Other Essays

Also available in Harvest paperback editions

C. S. Lewis at the Breakfast Table and Other Reminiscences,
edited by James T. Como
C. S. Lewis: A Biography,
by Roger Lancelyn Green and Walter Hooper
The Literary Legacy of C. S. Lewis,
by Chad Walsh